THE RISE, THE FALL AND THE _____ OF AMERICA!

THE RISE, THE FALL AND THE _____ OF AMERICA!

RAY LEPAGE

Printed by CreateSpace, an Amazon.com Company

DEDICATION

This my first book, which may be my last, is dedicated to my amazing wife and my family.

It is especially dedicated to my second-favorite country in the world, the United States of America—to its people who have yet to become all that God has meant them to be, to a country that has more potential to impact the world than any other, and to its leaders, who need to care more about the people they serve than they do about the lobbyists and the next election.

To my grandsons, Noah and Julien, and to the other grandchildren of Canada and America and the world, may you get to grow up in a better world because America chose to learn from the past and lead the world into a better future, not just for themselves alone but for all humanity!

CONTENTS

ACKNOWLEDGMENTS

Thank you to my wife of forty-five years, Sharon, for loving me through our challenging times and freeing me up to write this book as we enter retirement; to my son, Matthew, for his encouragement to get this book out; to my daughter, Lyndsay, for her help in the after-publishing marketing process; to my favorite daughter-in-law, Rhonda, for her layout work on the covers and the formatting of the images.

Thank you to Brian for his design, development, and management of our website; to Rae for his help on the initial material research; to Patsy for her support and encouragement.

Thank you to my friends at CreateSpace for their amazing help in the publishing of this book on my limited budget.

And thank you most of all to the God I try to serve. On most days, I attempt to do that better than I did the day before.

INTRODUCTION

How are we to measure a nation's greatness? By the good it does? Or by the evil, pain, and suffering it permits to happen?

All civilized countries do good.

America is not the greatest country in the world.

⊟⊨

Please do not read this book as a republican or democrat nor independent or even an American but as a citizen of the world.

As I struggle to complete the manuscript of this book, it is the summer of 2016. America is in the end stages of this presidential election cycle. You have been introduced to the Donald; I hope you are enjoying that ride.

Mr. Trump's motto is, *Make America Great Again.* May I respectfully suggest that, once you have read this book, you may understandably feel, that sadly, but honestly, America has never been, the greatest country in the world. Moving forward, it looks like it will be an all out battle between the Trump-Pence ticket, the Clinton-Kaine team, a libertarian party team of Johnson-Weld, and who knows who else, when all is said and done.

The television networks, social media and the candidates will continue to overwhelm you until November.

Both major candidates have significant negative ratings and one needs to wonder. Is this the best you can come up with, having to choose from over three hundred and thirty three million citizens?

You have had two conventions that to me, presented totally different visions for America. The first by the Republicans, a dark and negative view of America today and looking backwards. The second, by the Democrats, an upbeat, forward looking concept that we all hope for.

And then comes the election that has many countries fearful. My friends, you have brought all of this on yourselves.

❧

Pope Francis has recently completed his amazing trip to Cuba and the United States, bringing a message of humility, hope, and mercy.

The United Nations, that illustrious body of problem solvers, has just celebrated its seventieth anniversary, and most of the countries' leaders came to New York to speak. There, we were given a glimpse of what may lie ahead for this world if someone does not act—and act soon.

Violence in your cities abounds. Russia is flexing its muscles once again. ISIS is threatening the next global conflict. Can you say World War III?

Thus, the stage has been set for…*The Rise, the Fall, and the _____ of America*!

⊰⊱

"In the beginning, God created the heavens and the earth…God saw all that he had made and it was good" (Genesis 1:1, 31 NIV).

Now, even if you don't believe in creation, please indulge me and journey with me, at least for a while.

God created man and woman; it started out good, and that was the beginning of life on this planet. From that day onward, civilizations were formed and grew.

Now flip back to the front cover of this book and take a moment to look at the symbols portrayed there.

My friends, those are reminders to all of us of civilizations that have impacted society either as we know it now or as they were known then. All were made by humanity and, for all intents and purposes (and the main purpose of this book), are no more.

I would especially ask that you keep this next point in mind as we move forward. At the time these societies or civilizations existed, the leaders, creators, and indeed many (if not most) of the folks who lived in them, believed that they would exist forever. And for reasons way above my pay scale, they did not.

⊰⊱

Let's move forward, shall we, to 2025 and beyond. Can you picture a situation where America might not exist as we know it even today? It is certainly very different from what its founding fathers envisioned, isn't it? Can you picture it as a yet another failed society?

Now, any book or assignment is not worth the paper it is written on unless the reader is given some homework. Once you have read this book, make a copy of the cover, take a pen and fill in the missing word in the title. Choose well, my American friends. It is your future, the future of your children, the future of America, and indeed maybe that of the world we are talking about. Then go to your social media page and post it for others to see.

Speaking of social media, I would encourage you to go to your social media accounts and share your thoughts and ideas with your fellow Americans. I am sure you can be a blessing to each other and come up with some constructive solutions to what you are about to read.

And please do not waste your time going to our website at *www.whichwayamericanow.com*, to either thank me for the book or criticizing me for the same.

It's not about me; it's about you, the people, remember!

So, c'mon, America! Let's roll, and enjoy the journey!

Chapter 1

MY JOURNEY

I bring you warmest greetings from your neighbors in the Great White North, north of the forty-ninth parallel—north of Maine, New York, Wisconsin, and Montana!

I first sat down to write this book in January 2009 and have been struggling to get it finished.

It is now the summer of 2016, and I am thankful that life and recent events in America and around the world have given me pause to continue.

I needed the extra time to really take a close look at what my intentions were in writing this book and ensure that they were honorable, fair, and heartfelt.

My real journey begins on November 22, 1963, with the assassination of President John F. Kennedy.

Photo courtesy of the *Boston Herald.*

You see, I was an impressionable teenager at the time and was saddened the moment the announcement was made in my high school in Ottawa, Ontario, Canada. Over the next several days and weeks, the magnitude of this event started embedding itself in my spirit. I began to remember the joy and excitement my country had felt when the young president had been inaugurated just a couple of years earlier.

On the day of his funeral, I cried such tears of sadness.

In the ensuing years, when his name would come up on the anniversary of his death, I was saddened again. As I got older, I began to remember the hope that I and my country had had for this new president, a hope not just for America but for my own country and the rest of the world as well.

My friends, the day President Kennedy was laid to rest was the last time I cried for one of your presidents—that is, until

November 4, 2008, when the words "Obama Wins" were flashed across the CNN screen.

Photo courtesy of *Birmingham News*.

Now, you may think I am a Democrat, and you would be wrong. But hang in there!

You see, as a much older Canadian at this point, I had been following the entire election process very closely. And like so many Americans I have met, I don't know or even care very much about the difference between a liberal Democrat and a conservative Republican, a Tea-Partier or Libertarian or a Lou Dobbs Independent—and neither does the rest of the world.

In Canada's October 2015 election, we had five different parties and elected our prime minister with less than 40 percent of the popular vote and a voter turnout of 68 percent. His new cabinet has fifteen men and fifteen women.

But let me take you back to my recent tears for a moment. As I watched those words flash across the screen, we were presented with pictures of absolute celebration from various major cities around the world, and it was then that tears began to flow. Contrary to what my tears had been in 1963, these were tears of absolute joy. They were also tears of hope because the free world once again had hope that maybe, just maybe, America could and would now reach out and grasp for the God-given potential that it could have as a world leader.

You see, my friends, America never has been a *true* world leader. That title is something that has to be earned. It is nowhere near enough to say, "This is the greatest country in the world." Simply saying it does not make it so; it is either simple ignorance or, at the very least, arrogance.

As a concerned but hopeful outsider looking in, I hope and pray that this book can play a small role in opening the reader's eyes to both the potential positive role America could play and indeed the worst of America. Before America will be able to instill true leadership in this world, it must both acknowledge its horrific past and present, as presented in the following pages, and then show the world that it can right its ship and how it is going to do it. The world is waiting, but it can't wait much longer.

During my recent years living in Arizona, I came to realize that Americans live on the sound bites of any particular day.

They hear about violence, the health-care system, education, election cycles, climate change, and foreign policy. They hear it as a smattering of news but can't quite seem to piece it all together and determine for themselves what the state of their country is. As President Ford once said in a State of the Union message, "The state of the union is not good."

Life is too busy and overwhelming for most to keep up with it.

My desire is to give you that outsider's perspective from someone who is representative of so many people in the world who look toward America.

The wish of the founding fathers who sat down in Philadelphia so many years ago was indeed for their new nation to be the greatest country in the world.

I have written this as one who is and always has been a huge fan of your country, and, truth be told, I have more American friends than Canadian ones. I have traveled to over fifteen countries and been to more states and territories (forty-five) than most Americans. I am one who wishes for your children and grandchildren to live in a society that is an example of what it ought to be.

I remember vividly as a young person traveling to Italy, Norway, Sweden, Finland, the Netherlands, and the Congo in the late 1960s with friends from America and over twenty different countries. I especially remember being treated better because the flag on my backpack or luggage was Canadian and not American.

Then, over the years as an adult, I traveled to Mexico, Jamaica, St. Thomas, St. Marten, the Dominican Republic,

Cuba, Antigua, St. John, and even Puerto Rico and received more respect because I was not a "gringo."

And, finally, a few short years ago, an American friend of mine asked her husband if he wanted to go to the Holy Land. His answer was, "I'd love to, but they don't like us there." They stayed home.

Those events were eye-openers to me in the sense that they made me aware of what was and has really been happening not just *to* America but *in* America.

As we spend time together in these pages, I shall leave you with a question that I hope you can answer and that I will address in the last chapter of this book: Which way, America, are you going to go? The decision is all yours.

⊣⊢

Now, as you have no doubt noticed, the title of the book contains a blank space that only America and Americans can fill in. What will that space say in the generations to come?

The world is watching, my friends.

Do you even care?

The world continues to hope.

Does it matter to you at all?

I, for one, believe most Americans do care and would like for America to be accepted as the greatest country in the world.

So I invite you to join me on our journey. Just as this was difficult to write, it is not going to be pleasant to read and digest. I am just an average person who has spent most of my life wondering and hoping.

I don't have all the answers to give you in this book; Americans already have those. Some will disagree with my premise, and some will be upset, but like all Americans, all Canadians have free speech as well.

At the end of several chapters, you will find a challenge that I trust you will at least consider undertaking. Some are easier than others, but all are meant to challenge your soul and mind to impact your community and country even in a small way.

At the very end of the book, I have set aside a page per chapter for you to put down your thoughts and ideas as they might relate to that challenge.

One of my heroes President John F. Kennedy once said, "Ask not what your country can do for you; ask what you can do for your country."

I hope you will decide on what you can truly do as a concerned citizen to stop the downward spiral, turn things around, and set the bar higher for all your citizens.

It is my sincere desire that as you read these words, you will understand and respect what I am trying to convey. I have tried to pen them as I think and speak, and I hope my editors will respect that as well.

This book is small in the number of pages in comparison to typical books; I could have written a lot more. I could have given you more stats and charts on things like the environment, energy consumption, infrastructure, personal spending habits and any of several other topics, but that would have served no additional useful purpose. You'll understand why by the end of our time together.

My efforts are truly not meant for your scholars or politicians but rather for the average American who is seeing his or her white-picket-fence dream go down the proverbial tube and thinking he or she can't do anything about it.

C'mon, America! You can do this!

Chapter 2

THE AMERICAN DREAM

Let's begin this chapter by pausing for a few moments and writing down what you believe the American dream to be for you and your family today. You can make note of this on this chapter's notes page in the back of the book.

What was it like ten, twenty, thirty or even 50 years ago? What are your hopes and expectations for tomorrow and for the future for both you and your country?

James Truslow Adams defined the American dream in his book *The Epic of America*, written in 1931; he stated it is that dream of a land in which life should be better and richer and fuller for everyone, with opportunity for each according to his or her ability or achievement. It is a difficult dream for the European upper classes to interpret adequately, and too many of us ourselves have grown weary and mistrustful of it. It is not a dream of motor cars and high wages merely but of social order in which each man and each woman is able to attain the fullest stature of which they are innately capable and be recognized by others for what they are, regardless of the fortuitous circumstances of birth or position.

Three cheers for James Truslow Adams!

Or was it the homesteaders who left the eastern states and went west and south in the pursuit of that piece of land, taking advantage of their unalienable rights?

Or was it the immigrants who left their home countries, looking for a better country in their pursuit of liberty and happiness?

Or could it be a World War II soldier whose desire upon coming home was to have an education, a home, that white picket fence, a family, a job for life, and a car?

Or did the first concept of the American dream originate from the Declaration of Independence where the founding fathers "[held certain] truths to be self-evident, that all men are created equal, that they are endowed by their Creator with certain unalienable Rights, that among these are Life, Liberty and the Pursuit of Happiness"?

Or, sadly, has the American dream boiled down to material prosperity? What did happen to that little house with a white picket fence? Where is the job for life for Mom or Dad if he or she wanted that? Where is the neighborhood where the kids played safely in the street late into nighttime darkness? What happened to all of that simple yet possible American dream?

I respectfully suggest that the American dream has become the American greed and nightmare—where for so many years "keeping up with the Joneses" was a buzz phrase, but the Joneses have now lost their homes and moved back from whence they came. By the way, has anyone seen the Jones family lately? Some of them don't even have the picket-fence part of the dream.

Is it a place where the Jefferson's, who had moved on up to the east side, have packed the moving truck and headed back to the old neighborhood?

In the last several years, so many of you have lost your jobs, your homes, your IRAs, and your hope because that American dream was probably a figment of someone's imagination. What happened, and how did it happen so quickly?

Truth be told, it did not happen so quickly. It has been brewing for many years as people sought the brass ring, the big homes, early retirement, and all of the toys that the television, radio, print, and Internet ads said you just *needed* to have. But the blame does not stop there.

Let me put it where I think it primarily belongs from my perspective: Wall Street, greedy banks, insurance companies, and especially your federal government—which was asleep at the switch. They saw it coming but failed to react quickly enough, if at all.

They are the main reasons for the recent collapse of the world economy and downward spiral of the American psyche and morale, in my humble opinion—more profits for the insurance companies, more profits for investment banks, more profits for their traders, and more profits for their shareholders. And who are their shareholders? Middle and upper-class Americans!

When is enough stuff enough? Living in a modest house was just not good enough! Driving a midsized car was not good enough! Going to a good state university instead of the more prestigious ones was not enough. So many simply wanted more and were not satisfied with what they had.

They might have even been satisfied and excited about their initial retirement investment plan at one point, but along came an opportunity they could not or would not pass up.

The recent economic collapse is a perfect example of personal and corporate greed ruining the lives of countless Americans. The loss of your homes, jobs, and retirement funds is a serious matter. All of you know that by now, but let me share the bigger picture with you.

What America has permitted to happen has also affected the Canadian dream, the British dream, the Australian dream, the European dream, the Asian dream, the South American dream, and the African dream.

And many Americans would say, "Who cares?"

Well, my friends, I believe you should have cared and had better care moving forward, because, in this global landscape, it is no longer just about you—as you have thought for way too many years.

We Canadians were thankfully nowhere near as deeply affected by the recent economic crisis because our dream is not as grand and our banking system and Bay Street are well regulated. But what do we know? We are just those nice neighbors to the north where it's cold in the winter. Cold? It's fifty degrees here today in the Toronto area and twenty degrees in Boise!

How sad it was to see those retiring—or retired—folks lose absolutely everything through no fault of their own because of truly unscrupulous investment bankers and investment advisers.

And if you check very carefully, my friends, those same Wall Street folks and bankers will retire well.

Remember Bernie Madoff, a.k.a., I-Made-Off-with-Your-Money? He was also a very good indication of a more serious problem in America; I believe he may be the only well-known crook who went to jail.

❦

Well, as we move forward into 2016, the Dow is back to where it was before the bubble burst and beyond, before the recent oil price tumble and the problems in China, but I suspect the next Wall Street generation is hard at work yet again.

I wonder if anyone is watching that store these days. Do you care enough to find out and ask your congressional representatives?

❦

So now what's the next American dream going to look like?

How about going back to where all people are created equal for starters? How about regaining the values you claim to have?

How about making it possible for more people to afford that house with the picket fence?

How about making sure the people who live in that house can afford to go to college and be guaranteed a sound health system and a safe retirement?

CHALLENGE

The first part of this first challenge, my friends, is to give thanks for what you already have and work to keep it. Never mind the Joneses.

Don't risk your family's security or your retirement for the brass ring that simply is not there. Realize that if it is there, it may not last long.

Go ahead and dream big dreams for yourself, your family, and your country, but make sure they are based on some sense of reality.

Write down what your dream of America looks like for your family in the next ten years.

What does your dream look like for your country in the next ten to twenty years?

Encourage others to do the same and journey with them to help each other through the bad times and rejoice in the good. Isn't that supposed to be the American way?

Chapter 3

OF EMPIRES AND AMERICA

Over these past many centuries, several dominant societies, empires, and dictatorships have come and gone, while a few are only glimmers of what they once were. As I was searching for information on those people groups, I wondered if the founders, leaders, and originators of those societies fervently believed that they would last forever. May I respectfully suggest that their egos were big enough for them to believe that what they had created would indeed last until the end of time.

Let me share with you some past examples and let you judge for yourselves.

Period Name	Date began	Date ended	Duration in years
Roman	27 BC	AD 476	503
Ottoman	AD 1293	1923	630
French Aristocracy	1440	1790	350
British	1497	1997	500
United States	1776	TBD	TBD
Japanese	1868	1945	77
Soviet Communists	1917	1990s	73
Nazi Germany	1933	1945	12
ISIS	2004	TBD	TBD

As you can clearly see, some of these lasted for many years, even centuries, and in most cases, arguably way too long. A little history of America and commentary is appropriate at this point.

THE REVOLUTIONARY WAR (APRIL 19, 1775, TO SEPTEMBER 3, 1783)

A war started it all, and, sadly, the new nation's foundation was built on violence. Was it justified against an oppressive British regime? Certainly, but that may have set the groundwork, the mind-set, and the justification for future wars down the road in the nation's history.

Actually, this war was preceded by the arrival of the Pilgrims on the *Mayflower* at Plymouth Rock in 1620. And that event, my friends, was not the settlement of a nation by Europeans but the invasion of a nation already inhabited for centuries by an entire civilization.

THE CIVIL WAR (APRIL 12, 1861, TO APRIL 9, 1865)

These were some of the darkest times in American history when Americans were fighting Americans over Americans.

It was a war in which over 620,000 men lost their lives in battle, approximately 2 percent of the population of the day. In today's numbers, that would amount to over six million brave souls.

For every three soldiers who died in battle, five more died of disease. That 620,000 compares to over 400,000 in World War II and more than 116,000 in World War I. [1]

And more than 150 years later, racism still exists in America, both in real, everyday life and in the spirits of way too many. Arguably, your greatest president paid the price with his life but did leave a legacy for other presidents and Americans to build upon and protect.

How would President Lincoln feel if he were here today and saw the state of racism in America, not just against blacks but other immigrant people groups and native people? May I respectfully suggest he would be devastated and feel that the Civil War had been all for naught.

THE AMERICAN INDIAN WARS (1622 THROUGH 1890 (INTERMITTENT) TO PRESENT)

I would direct your attention to the dates in the heading since this is how long America's first citizens have been struggling, beginning two years after the *Mayflower*. They long ago lost their dream to thrive and, truth be told, are barely surviving today.

---

1   http://www.militaryfactory.com/american_war_deaths.asp

The white men in Washington and settlers to the West and South made sure of that many years ago.

What you have done to these fellow countrymen over centuries is shameful. A good indication of that has been Hollywood's portrayal of these Native Americans in movies over the years— movies like *Stagecoach* (1939), *They Died with Their Boots On* (1941), *Fort Apache* (1958), and *The Searchers* (1956).

The spirit of the American Indian was broken long ago, and it is probably too late to rekindle it, given the days we live in.

Can you believe this mistreatment of Native Americans was permitted to happen by the greatest country in the world?

Their lands are long gone, their present living conditions are atrocious for the most part, and they have little or no voice in government with presently only two members in the 113th Congress. You even had the nerve to pass the Indian Removal Act of 1830. That act gave President Andrew Jackson the power to grant unsettled lands west of the Mississippi in exchange for Indian lands within existing state borders. A few tribes went peacefully, but during the fall and winter of 1838 and 1839, the Cherokees were forcibly moved west by the government. Approximately four thousand of them died on this forced march, which became known as the Trail of Tears. Bet you did not know that one.

Folks! The time for playing cowboys and Indians is long over!

WORLD WAR I (JULY 28, 1914, TO NOVEMBER 11, 1918)
"The war to end all wars."

America, in its infinite wisdom and protectionist/isolationist attitude, entered the Great War on April 6, 1917, a full thirty-two months after it began. Here are a couple of questions for your consideration.

How much sooner would the war have ended, and how many lives would have been spared if America had entered sooner?

You went in late; the world wins! Hold that thought! I do have a point coming.

WORLD WAR II (SEPTEMBER 1, 1939, TO SEPTEMBER 2, 1945)

America, again in its infinite wisdom and protectionist attitude, entered this second "great" war on December 7, 1941, a full twenty-seven months after it began. Granted, it did provide material and logistical support earlier on.

Here are the same two questions for your consideration. How much sooner would the war have ended, and how many lives would have been spared if America had acted sooner?

You went in late; the world wins! Hang in there—my point is coming!

This was a war America was forced into after an attack on its own soil, and then as an ally of other nations already involved. America contributed to the fight and the end. Contrary to what movies show and most people in America believe, America did not win the war by itself.

Now, my friends, the real cost of human sacrifice in this war was not only the six million Jews and tens of thousands of soldiers who died on all sides. The real sacrifices were made by the civilian population in the countries that were invaded or where battles were fought. But I don't recall having heard much of that over the years.

Look at the following chart closely and see the amount of human suffering caused to not only this number of civilians but to their families and to the fabric of those nations. Some countries would never be the same again.

Allies	Civilian Deaths
Great Britain and Commonwealth	60,000
France	360,000
United States	68 at Pearl Harbor plus 6 on mainland
USSR	7,700,000
Belgium	90,000
Holland	190,000
Poland	5,300,000
Greece	80,000
Yugoslavia	1,300,000
Czechoslovakia	330,000
Axis Powers	
Germany	3,810,000
Austria	80,000
Italy	85,000
Romania	465,000
Hungary	280,000
Japan	360,000

THE KOREAN CONFLICT (JUNE 25, 1950, TO JULY 27, 1953)

The United States provided the bulk of the manpower and armaments for this conflict between North Korea/China/Russia and a United Nations military alliance of twenty-one nations.

After many incursions deep into South Korea, the aggressors were pushed back to the thirty-eighth parallel, a demilitarized zone was created, and an armistice was signed that stands to this day.

The present-day challenge is to control a crazy dictator with his hand on a nuclear button, a massive fanatical and brainwashed army, and a dirt-poor civilian population. America still has a large military presence there.

THE VIETNAM WAR (NOVEMBER 1, 1955, TO APRIL 30, 1975)

This was an unwanted war where a superpower nation invaded a small country and lost. It not only lost the war but allowed returning soldiers to be ignored, reviled, or ridiculed by its people and forgotten by the government even to this day.

Selective service was very selective as to who got deferments. You can check into it on your own if you care to, and you will be appalled.

You gave up over fifty thousand of your bravest and trillions of dollars and lost it all, because might did not make right any more then than it did before Vietnam, during Vietnam, or now.

You went in at the beginning and lost the war!

THE GULF WAR (AUGUST 2, 1990, TO FEBRUARY 28, 1991) / OPERATION DESERT STORM (JANUARY 17 TO FEBRUARY 28, 1991) AND TURNS INTO THE IRAQ WAR

America was part of a coalition of thirty-four nations that attacked Iraq in response to Iraq's invasion of Kuwait and to defend Saudi Arabia.

It is now America's longest war because you reentered twenty years later, and you won't be coming out anytime soon either.

You went in at the beginning and are losing the war!

AMERICA UNDER ATTACK (SEPTEMBER 11, 2001)

President Roosevelt in his speech to Congress after Pearl Harbor commented that the day of that attack would be "a day that will go down in infamy." Well, I am not sure about infamy unless you consider the dropping of the atomic bomb infamy as well. (By the way, I would have supported the dropping of those two bombs.)

As for 9/11, it was indeed a terrible day for America and for countries that lost citizens. Certainly, it was an infamous day and, as it turns out, a life-changing day for the entire world as well.

We are now almost fifteen years out, and the real impact of the aftermath of 9/11 is coming home to roost. The invasion of Iraq and the war in Afghanistan has awakened an enemy, an enemy your country and the world never saw coming, just like they didn't see the 9/11 attackers coming, although there were signs.

How's that for the greatest country in the world?

As an aside (but an important one), I was truly disappointed in the immediate aftermath of this event, at not seeing the American Muslim community stand up by the tens of thousands and denounce what had just happened. If there had been such a thing as a Million Muslim Person March, what an impact that would have had then and maybe even to this day.

Or, heaven forbid, what if our Muslim allies around the world would have taken a very public stance against this horrible event? (And, by the way, heaven wouldn't forbid it!)

AFGHANISTAN WAR (OCTOBER 7, 2001, TO DECEMBER 28, 2014, AND ONGOING)

Afghanistan is the very same country that the Russians had tried to deal with years before and left with their tails between their legs. I am simply guessing that America just had to prove they could do better than the Russians did. And how did that work out?

This recent war took thirteen years and resolved nothing. President Obama has been forced to leave 8,500 troops as of this summer in this fruitless endeavor. This country continues to be a hotbed of Muslim fanaticism, helping raise the future generations of terrorists. This was a war in which my countrymen served and died alongside American and coalition soldiers.

Unfortunately, another small country kicked your butts at tremendous sacrifice to so many.

You went in at the beginning and lost the war!

THE IRAQI WAR (MARCH 20, 2003, TO DECEMBER 2011 (COMBAT TROOP WITHDRAWAL) AND ONGOING

Initiated by misinformation and a false sense of what a Bush administration felt it needed to do to either save face or remind the world once again of America's might.

American fighting forces have left the country in the hands of corrupt politicians and untrained soldiers with no desire to fight. Last time I looked, most of the material left behind by Americans, worth billions of dollars, has now been acquired by the enemy.

Now, that is strategic planning at the highest level.

You went in at the beginning and will lose the war!

That point I have been alluding to for a few sections—here it is, point made!

But we are not done yet! As of this writing, a small contingent of adviser/combat troops is headed back. Stay tuned!

WORLD WAR III (THE WAR AGAINST ISIS) (NOVEMBER 13, 2015, UNTIL GOD KNOWS WHEN)

A case can be made that this war against ISIS fomented several years ago on the night of 9/11, when President Bush asked his team to find some evidence that Iraq was somehow responsible for the attacks on America.

It is a war that began with the US invasion of Iraq and Afghanistan, a war where America was joined in the early stages, at least in Afghanistan, by skeptical and sometimes unwilling allies, a war where little or no thought was given to what would happen when Saddam Hussein was removed.

In 2003, the United States set up Camp Bucca in Iraq and detained almost twenty thousand Jihadi men.

During their stay there, most of them were radicalized right in front of their American captors. The present-day leader of ISIS, Abu Bakr al-Baghdadi, was one of the detainees and was let go because he was believed by the Americans to be someone they could work with.

In recent months, a Russian passenger jet was blown out of the sky, a bomb in a Libyan market killed over forty people, a homegrown terrorist killed many in San Bernardino, and more than one hundred thirty innocent people were murdered in Paris.

French president Hollande, speaking as the first president since World War II to address both houses of his government commented, "This is war." " And that Paris attack was followed by two vicious attacks at a Brussels airport and train station.

America and the world are once again at one of those defining moments in history. Make no mistake, this battle is not a religious one but one of ideology, much like the Second World War was about Nazism taking over the world.

The one good thing about World War II was that it was fought by armies against armies. This one will be fought against lone wolves or groups of radical Islamic terrorists who have absolutely no respect for our values or human life. Yes, I watched the video of their burning a young man alive in a cage!

In the aftermath of the Paris massacre, I am still waiting for the Muslim communities of the world to hold that Million Muslim March to support world freedoms.

I am still waiting for the Muslim countries to join in the fight.

I am still waiting for the Muslim countries to open their doors and take in the major share of Syrian refugees, a group that is, no doubt, infiltrated by potential terrorists sneaking into Europe and Canada and beyond.

I am still waiting for the Muslim leaders to confirm to the terrorists over the television stations of the world (including Al Jazeera), that there is *no* paradise awaiting them and the 72 virgins have been called away and won't be there either. Actually, it appears the proper translation relating to the virgins is the word raisin.

And then, there was Orlando!

RACIAL SEGREGATION AND HUMAN RIGHTS

Sadly, I could not put this section in any chronological order since this conflict has been going on for centuries and continues today. Entire books and school curricula have been written on this subject by much smarter people, so I'll just pass on a few observations.

Not only did America not respect its initial citizens going back to 1622, but it had to go overseas to Africa and bring in a labor force that would be abused to this day. Not enough willing white guys to do the work back then, I guess!

And now, in recent years, you still can't get enough white people to do the needed labor, so you get them from Mexico and Latin America.

Then you watch TV shows on crime like *First 48* that we will talk about later where most of the criminals presented there are either black or Latino.

What does that tell you about those people groups, or better yet, what does it tell them as they sit and watch? Do the white viewers sit there all smug and say, "See, look at those…" And how do you think our black and Latino friends feel seeing themselves portrayed like that day in and day out?

Remember the racial strife of the late sixties? I read somewhere that "all men are created equal" Well! All men were not treated equal in those days for sure. Those were horrible, gut-wrenching times for America, and very visible signs still persist to this day.

At a recent Red Sox baseball game, where Jackie Robinson was remembered, a Baltimore outfielder was called racial slurs by several culturally challenged fans including the "n" word.

As I traveled in the South and other parts of America in recent years, I was an outsider; I could see and feel the negative sentiments still existing in many areas of society.

One vivid example was that of having a meal with friends at a major restaurant where our server was a young black man. He did an amazing job for us, and as we were walking to our cars, I commented on the great service. My host's response almost floored me. Coming from a wonderful, godly person were these words: "Yes, he did! We do have some good n—s in the South!" I am still feeling the pain I felt as I write this now, years later.

So much has been written about Dr. Martin Luther King Jr., the work of his movement, and the amazing impact he has had on your society. He is definitely one of my own American heroes! Whatever happened to him?

On the human rights side, let me draw your attention to the fact that this great nation did not permit women to fully vote until 1920. What was up with that? And some states even withdrew the women's right to vote altogether back in that time period. That's one more tidbit most of you probably did not know about.

For your black brothers and sisters, it wasn't until Congress passed the Voting Rights Act of 1965 pursuant to Section 2 of the Fifteenth Amendment that they were truly and more easily able to cast a vote. For decades, state legislatures had put stumbling blocks in their way.

By 1976, 63 percent of Southern blacks were registered to vote, and at that time, that was only 5 percent less than Southern whites. Finally, they were getting there, right?

And two summers ago in Wilcox County Georgia, the first non-segregated prom in decades was held. Really?

⧊⧊

And finally, in a recent report from the US Government Accountability Office (GAO) investigators found the following looking at the school years from 2000-2001 to the 2013-2014 school year.

Both the percentage of K-12 public schools in high-poverty and the percentage comprised of mostly African-American or Hispanic students grew significantly, more than doubling, from 7,009 schools to 15,089 schools. They also found the percentage of all schools with so-called racial or socio-economic isolation grew from 9% to 16%.

⧊⧊

On a recent trip to the United States, my wife and I were at the Atlanta airport, waiting for a flight to Louisiana. As we sat down, we noticed a couple of toddlers playing nearby and having a great time chasing each other around the waiting area. It continued much to the parents' delight or frustration at having to reel them back in.

And then it hit me! One was Asian and the other African American, and those two cute little people couldn't care less about the color of each other's skin. After we chatted with the parents, we found out that neither did they. There is hope!

The last thing this old world needs is yet another failed society, especially a society with more potential than the ones that came and went before. Please do not permit history to put a fail date in the chart at the beginning of this chapter. Your grandchildren and the grandchildren of the entire world deserve a better fate and better ending to the not-yet-great American story.

CHALLENGE

In this challenge, I am going to ask you to sit back, evaluate, and write down what part you may have played or are currently playing in the decay of America. If truth be told, all of you have had a role to play, a role either by commission or omission.

Talk to your family and friends and ask them what they think and what they could be doing individually or as a group. Talk about the reality that the total demise of America may very well happen, and challenge them to face that possibility down the road. And work to do something—if not for yourselves, then for the next generations of Americans and the rest of the world!

My friends, I believe I am doing something by writing this book, and I am not even a citizen of America. I may not be, but I am a citizen of the world and not going to leave this earth without trying to help out.

There is more than *me*, myself, and I at stake.

Chapter 4

HERE'S LOOKING AT YOU!

E very day around the world, people will read a newspaper, listen to a radio, turn on the TV, or go to the Internet to find
out what's happening in America. And they hope!

Sadly, what they see or hear is not good or encouraging, and
millions are disappointed.

In this chapter, I would like to share with you some of the
things people do see coming out of America.

And many of those people are watching live on Main Street,
America!

ON INCOME INEQUALITY

Why is it that in the greatest country in the world, one-tenth of 1
percent of the people own as much wealth as the other 90 percent

of people, while twenty-seven million people live in poverty? I sound just like Bernie Sanders![2]

Almost half of the members of congress have a net worth of over $1 million. [3]

The payroll of all your four professional sports leagues is greater than the GDP of over 60 countries. I'm not kidding here! [4][5][6][7][8]

Now, I don't mind wealth; I have had some and wouldn't mind having some again.

By the way, we lost our home in Alberta in the Wall Street greed of 2008. We also lost our savings because of medical bills during our recent stay in Arizona. Is this section just sour grapes? Not really—it just makes for good first-person and personal book material. The sad part is that countless millions of your own people suffered and continue to suffer the same fate.

---

2   National Bureau of Economic Research, October 2014. Emmanuel Saez, Gabriel Zucman

3   http://www.opensecrets.org/news/2015/01/one-member-of-congress-18-american-households-lawmakers-personal-finances-far-from-average/

4   MLB: http://deadspin.com/2015-payrolls-and-salaries-for-every-mlb-team-1695040045

5   NFL: https://www.nflpa.com/news/all-news/2015-nfl-salary-cap-and-adjusted-team-positions

6   NBA: http://www.basketball-reference.com/contracts/

7   NHL: http://www.nhlpa.com/the-players/team-compensation

8   http://statisticstimes.com/economy/countries-by-projected-gdp.php

ON NATIONAL FEDERAL DEBT

Are you ready for this? Best get a big piece of paper! Drum roll, please!

Over $19.2 trillion is your national debt, or $55,000 right now for every man woman and child. This probably will blow past $20 trillion before election time at the end of this year! Family of four—you do the math!

Isn't this quite a legacy to leave your grandkids and great-grandkids and great-great-grandkids? And that is just the federal debt, folks. Go check out the state, local, and personal debt load yourselves. Or better yet, I dare you to go to usdebtclock.org, but be prepared to take your heart medicine.

Sadly, my friends, this is not showing any signs of slowing down. Who will get to pay for it? Very little of it, if any, will be paid for by the people who created it.

According to the US Treasury, in 2014, the largest domestic owner of US debt is Social Security at 16 percent, followed by other federal government entities at 13 percent, and the Federal Reserve at 12 percent.

How much of that debt is owned by foreign governments? In total, they own 34.4 percent, led by China at 7.2 percent and Japan at 7 percent. The balance is taken up by other countries, including oil exporters and countries that are not friendly to America.

ON THE MILITARY

No doubt the most powerful nation in the history of the world has some of the bravest soldiers to serve in its military. But with that comes both a fiscal and moral responsibility to its people and a needy world.

In 2014, America spent $581 billion dollars on its military (which works out to $1,821.00 for every man, woman, and child every year). According to the Pentagon's accounting of US military bases around the world, America has 662 bases in 38 countries (Pentagon *Base Structure Report, Fiscal 2010*). Do you really need that many bases and, if so, why? To protect the world? Really!

As for actual personnel, a September 30, 2010, Pentagon document titled Active Duty Military Personnel Strengths by Regional Area and by Country reported at least one member of the US military on the ground in 148 countries.

In 56 of these 148 countries, however, the United States has fewer than ten active-duty personnel present. These include such obscure locales as Mongolia, Nepal, Gabon, Togo, and Suriname.

But more important, what might have happened to all of the soldiers who have given up their lives in some of America's needless and fruitless interventions? What might have become of them?

That question came to mind on a recent stop at that same Atlanta airport where I saw a young soldier walk by. I actually wondered what would happen to him.

I also wondered why he joined the military. Was it out of a sense of service, which is truly admirable? Or was it maybe because he couldn't find a job or possibly could not afford an education, and this was a way to do that for himself?

CHART ON YEARLY MILITARY SPENDING

(from the International Institute for Strategic Studies 2015) (www.iiss.org)

Military Spending 2015	Billions of Dollars
United States	598
China	146
Saudi Arabia	82
Russia	52
United Kingdom	56
France	32
Japan	41
India	48
Germany	37
South Korea	33
Total (nonUSA)	527

GRAPH ON YEARLY MILITARY SPENDING IN BILLIONS

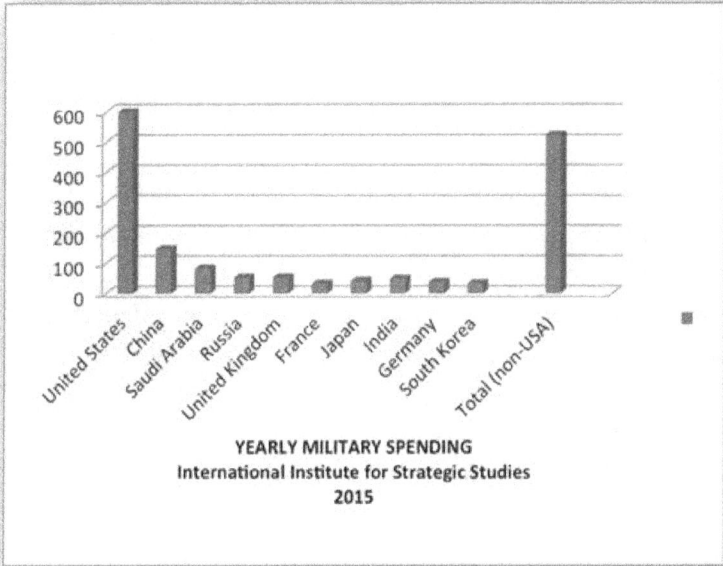

YEARLY MILITARY SPENDING
International Institute for Strategic Studies
2015

ON COLLEGE DEBT

Your 2014 graduating student had an average debt of $30,000. Makes the middle class and lower classes excited about the prospect of higher education and a good job, doesn't it? Look at the *PISA* education report that is coming up and see where you stand as a country. And please don't forget the $400 million in student-debt default. This is your country's future we are talking about here.

PETS VERSUS WOMEN'S SHELTERS

Granted you will find this a weird category but it just came to mind one day.

Why is it that in most cities, there is more real estate space allocated for pet supplies and animal medical facilities combined than there are for women's shelters? My friends, I am not sure this one needs any more explanation.

And then, according to the SPCA, there are 13,600 independent community animal shelters that receive 7.6 million animals annually. Of those, over 2.6 million are euthanized. You have 70 to 80 million dogs and 74 to 96 million cats. Only 10 percent of the animals received by shelters have been spayed or neutered, while 83 percent of pet dogs and 91 percent of pet cats are spayed or neutered.

Folks! As Bob Barker from television fame was known for saying, "Please get your pets spayed or neutered." Please care enough for your animals so that they can care for your family. [9]

ON GOVERNMENT

As I mentioned at the opening of the book, it was President Obama's presidential victory that finally got me off the couch and onto writing this book, which has been stirring in my spirit for years.

How much truth is there in the following statement? "Your elected official's next election campaign begins the day after last night's victory." You may have presidential elections every four

---

9 ASPCA: http://www.aspca.org/animal-homelessness/shelter-intake-and-surrender/pet-statistics

years and congressional elections every two years, but I swear, the world thinks you are always in election mode.

And as you moved into your conventions this summer, it appeared you were headed into troubling waters. The issue of super delegates on the Democratic side and a Republican party ready to disintegrate, will no doubt cause the citizenry to be concerned and fearful. You could have all been drawn back to the convention of 1968 in Chicago and the chaos of those days. Thankfully, cooler heads prevailed.

Backroom deals are being planned as we speak between now and election night but don't worry.

That is nothing new for America my friends.

If you have not done so, do take the time to watch the CNN series, *Race to the White House*, I recently did, enjoyed it, and was amazed but not surprised to learn about your political past.

In my country, with a land and water mass larger than that of the United States and a five-party system, election campaigns last forty-five to seventy-eight days, and our costs are around $50,000.000. Remember that number!

We have managed in almost 150 years since confederation to get it done; it works for us, and we are *not* the best country in the world. (I can't believe I said that!)

The American Congress votes are mostly based on what the party thinks at the time and whether that position will get them reelected or not. Votes are not focused on what the right thing might be for the country. Sure, many will sometimes vote their consciences, but more often than not, they are to vote along party lines.

I do not pretend to understand all of the workings of your government, but, then again, most Americans don't either. Yet, on the final House vote on the health-care bill in March 2010, all of the Republicans voted one way and most Democrats the other. At least there were some Democrats who voted against the party's wishes.

I came to the conclusion, right or wrong, that the Republicans realized that the health-care bill was going to pass. This being the most important piece of legislation in fifty years, they were determined that *their* name was not going to be on it. It would have been done by a Democratic president and a Democratic Congress. I could see no other reason. Can you?

❦

As a matter of general interest, here are the occupations of previous presidents, before serving as president. Twenty-eight presidents were lawyers, and eight were soldiers.[10]

---

10 http://www.infoplease.com/ipa/A0768854.html

President	Major Jobs before the Presidency
George Washington	surveyor, planter, general of the Army of the United Colonies
John Adams	schoolteacher, lawyer, diplomat, vice president under Washington
Thomas Jefferson	writer, inventor, lawyer, architect, governor of Virginia, secretary of state under Washington, vice president under Adams
James Madison	lawyer, political theorist, US congressman, secretary of state under Jefferson
James Monroe	soldier, lawyer, US senator, governor of Virginia
John Quincy Adams	lawyer, diplomat, professor, US senator, secretary of state under Monroe
Andrew Jackson	soldier, US congressman, US senator, governor of Florida
Martin Van Buren	lawyer, US senator, governor of New York, vice president under Jackson
William Harrison	soldier, diplomat, US congressman, US senator from Ohio
John Tyler	lawyer, US congressman, US senator, vice president under Harrison

James Polk	lawyer, US congressman, governor of Tennessee
Zachary Taylor	soldier
Millard Fillmore	lawyer, US congressman, vice president under Taylor
Franklin Pierce	lawyer, soldier, US congressman, US senator from New Hampshire
James Buchanan	lawyer, US congressman, US senator, US secretary of state
Abraham Lincoln	postmaster, lawyer, US congressman from Illinois
Andrew Johnson	tailor, US congressman, governor of Tennessee, US senator from Tennessee, vice president under Lincoln
Ulysses Grant	US Army general
Rutherford Hayes	lawyer, soldier, US congressman, governor of Ohio
James Garfield	schoolteacher, soldier, US representative from Ohio
Chester Arthur	schoolteacher, lawyer, tariff collector, vice president under Garfield
Grover Cleveland	sheriff, lawyer, mayor, governor of New York

Benjamin Harrison	lawyer, soldier, journalist, US senator from Indiana
William McKinley	soldier, lawyer, US congressman, governor of Ohio
Theodore Roosevelt	rancher, soldier, governor of New York, vice president under McKinley
William Taft	lawyer, judge, dean of the University of Cincinnati Law School, US secretary of war
Woodrow Wilson	lawyer, professor, president of Princeton University, governor of New Jersey
Warren Harding	newspaper editor, US senator from Ohio
Calvin Coolidge	lawyer, governor of Massachusetts, vice president under Harding
Herbert Hoover	engineer, US secretary of commerce
Franklin Roosevelt	lawyer, governor of New York
Harry Truman	farmer, soldier, haberdasher, judge, US senator, vice president under Roosevelt

Dwight Eisenhower	commander of the Allied forces in Europe, army chief of staff
John Kennedy	journalist, congressman, senator from Massachusetts
Lyndon Johnson	teacher, soldier, congressman, senator from Texas, vice president under Kennedy
Richard Nixon	lawyer, US congressman, US senator, vice president under Eisenhower
Gerald Ford	lawyer, US congressman, vice president under Nixon
Jimmy Carter	peanut farmer, governor of Georgia
Ronald Reagan	movie actor, corporate spokesman, governor of California
George Herbert Walker Bush	oil executive, US congressman, ambassador to the UN, CIA director, vice president under Reagan
William Clinton	lawyer, governor of Arkansas
George Walker Bush	oil executive, sports team owner, governor of Texas
Barack Obama	community organizer, civil rights lawyer, Illinois state senator, US senator

And then at this point, I thought you might be interested in seeing the previous occupations for members of the 113th Congress. See if you can pick up a trend here! Maybe, just maybe, a few too many lawyers! See the next chart

113TH CONGRESS

Previous Occupations	Representatives	Senators
Businesspeople	187	27
Educators	77	15
Lawyers	**156**	**55**

Although most countries in this world, including the democratic ones, aspire to the system both of our countries have, the greatness of America lies in its people and not its leaders or institutions or government.

Until you decide to send people to your state houses and Congress who are there for you (as in "for the people and by the people") rather than to get reelected or to grind a personal ax, substantive progress will never be made. It takes so much money and influence to get elected; the temptations to pander to lobbyists and big interest groups have to be challenging, if not impossible, to deal with.

I invite you to take the time, find the right government website, and see how many blue-collar workers—like teachers, nurses, and clerical workers—are presently in Congress.

ON THE COST OF ELECTIONS

I thought it would be useful to share information on the financial costs of the 2008 election, recognizing that the numbers for 2016 will be even greater, partly as a result of recent changes in donating rules. It didn't seem to make much sense for me to write it all when the following article has already clearly spelled it out. Special thanks to the Center for Responsive Politics and Open Secrets.org for their presentation.

US Election Will Cost $5.3 Billion, Center for Responsive Politics Predicts
Published by Communications on October 22, 2008, 10:20 p.m.
2008 contests for White House and Congress add up to the most expensive US election in history

WASHINGTON—The 2008 election for president and Congress is not only one of the most closely watched US elections in years; it's also the most expensive in history. The nonpartisan Center for Responsive Politics estimates that more than $5.3 billion will go toward the federal contests upcoming on Nov. 4.

The presidential race alone will cost nearly $2.4 billion, the Center predicts. Already the candidates alone have raised more than $1.5 billion since the election cycle's start in January 2007. This is the first time that candidates for the White House have raised and spent more than $1 billion, and this year's total is on track to nearly double candidate fundraising in 2004 and triple 2000.

Weeks before Election Day, the 2008 cycle has already surpassed $4.5 billion, $300 million more than the $4.2 billion that had been raised by the conclusion of the 2004 cycle. The overall estimated cost of the 2008 election would represent a 27 percent increase over the 2004 cycle. Looking at each party's growth, however, Democrats will have collected 52 percent more money for their congressional and presidential efforts by the end of this election cycle, compared to four years ago. Republican fundraising growth, however, has been a meager 2 percent since '04.

"This election will blow through historic records on a number of counts," said Sheila Krumholz, executive director of the Center for Responsive Politics. "We've marveled for years at the cost of elections, especially during presidential cycles, but this one is the first to cross the $5 billion mark. At the same time, it's encouraging to see more Americans than ever participating and offsetting the traditional dominance of special interests and wealthy donors who might be expecting payback. The only payback the small donor is expecting is a victory on Election Day. And that's healthier for our democracy."

The Center, which operates the award-winning website OpenSecrets.org and has been tracking the money financing federal elections since the 1980s, based its prediction of the 2008 election's overall cost on fundraising reported to the Federal Election Commission as of Oct. 21 by all candidates for federal office, political party committees and federally focused 527 committees. This conservative estimate also includes independent expenditures on advertising and get-out-the-vote efforts by outside political action committees to support and oppose candidates, and it includes public funding for presidential candidates and estimated fundraising by the host committees of the major parties' summer nominating conventions.

Industries, Companies Show Their Stripes
The money paying for the election—the home-stretch advertising, voter mobilization and other campaigning—is coming largely from the same industries and interests that have funded past elections. Topping the Center's 2008 list of big donors are contributors who list their occupation as "retired" (accounting for at least $204.3 million), lawyers and law firms ($180.9 million), the securities/investment industry ($122.8 million), real estate ($105.5 million) and health professionals ($69.6 million). Business interests account for about 72 percent of all contributions, with ideological, labor and other interests making up the rest.

"Among the big-giving industries, the Democrats' advantage is smaller than in the overall election," Krumholz said. "While lawyers remain strongly in the Democrats' camp and Wall Street favors them, too, some of the other top givers—retirees, real estate and doctors and other health professionals—are mostly split at this point between the two major parties. Democrats have solid support in a number of traditionally supportive industries, of course, including the entertainment industry and among college professors and other educators, but Republicans can count on contributions from the oil and gas, pharmaceutical and manufacturing industries."

Viewed more broadly, the finance, insurance and real estate sector once again dominates in political contributions, exceeding $373 million in the Center's most recent analysis. Democrats have a slight edge with the finance sector.

The top donors this cycle, based on contributions from their PACs and employees, is dominated by companies in the financial sector, and most of them favor Democrats.

After ActBlue, the online organization that directs individual contributions to progressive candidates, the top corporation in 2008 is once again Goldman Sachs. The global investment bank's employees and PAC have contributed at least $5 million to the '08 campaign. Citigroup is next at $4.2 million, followed by JPMorgan Chase & Co. at $4.1 million. The biggest-giving industry association is the National Association of Realtors, which has given nearly $3.2 million.

"Wall Street and other industries in the financial sector don't seem to have tightened their belts—no signs of recession in their political giving. Of course, their contributions may be part of a strategy to continue securing government assistance for their businesses as the economy heads further south," Krumholz said.

Incumbents and Democrats Have the Advantage

All candidates for House and Senate have raised more than $1.5 billion, based on data available from the FEC on Oct. 21. Incumbents running for reelection continue to have a huge advantage, the Center found.

The average Senate incumbent has raised $8.3 million (which includes money raised since the start of the six-year term in 2003) to the average challenger's $850,000, an advantage of nearly 10 to 1. For candidates looking to claim an open Senate seat, the average is about $1.6 million and varies widely depending on the state's size and advertising costs. The incumbent's advantage in the House is also lop-sided. Members of the House have raised approximately $1.2 million through the 3rd Quarter of this year, on average, while their opponents have raised an average of $286,000—a 4 to 1 edge for the seat holder. Open-seat candidates have collected about $497,000. Candidates for Congress in 2008 have spent nearly $95 million from their own pockets to get elected.

"You can't win a seat in Congress without being personally wealthy or knowing a lot of wealthy people who are willing to back you with their money," Krumholz said. "With Election Day coming up, it's important for candidates and citizens to Remember that you can't win without votes, either."

Democrats have outraised Republicans consistently throughout this election cycle, and overall it appears Democrats will end up collecting 59 percent of the money raised in '08. In 2004, there was a nearly even split between the parties.

"The Democrats' takeover of Congress in the 2006 election quickly shifted the fundraising advantage to their side. Money follows power," Krumholz said. "The Republican Party's longtime lead in the campaign finance game has been erased in this election, due to the Democrats' control of the congressional agenda and their side's more skillful use of online fundraising, especially in the presidential race."

If history is any guide, most congressional incumbents should expect to return to Washington next year. In the last five elections, since the 1998 contests, an average of 97 percent of House incumbents have won reelection, as have 86 percent of senators. Even two years ago, when control of Congress shifted to the Democratic Party, 94 percent of House members still won reelection as did 79 percent of senators.

Individual Donors Still Represent Tiny Slice Of America
The Center has identified more than 1 million individuals who have made a contribution of more than $200 to

federal candidates, parties and PACs, close to the 1.1 million individuals who showed up in FEC records in 2004. The total for 2008 (and for 2004, for that matter) is far higher, however, as only contributors giving more than $200 must be disclosed by name to the FEC.

In 2008, the number of itemized individuals still represents less than 0.5 percent of all adult Americans. Analysts have estimated that, historically, no more than 4 percent of Americans make a contribution of any size to federal politics.

By comparison, about 10 percent of American taxpayers elect to dedicate $3 of their annual tax bill to the presidential public financing system. Many new donors have been brought into the fold in 2008, but participation in this element of our democracy isn't representative of the electorate or the nation as a whole," Krumholz said. "The typical campaign contributor showing up in government data is still typically a lawyer, a Wall Street banker, a doctor, a CEO or a college professor at a major university.

For all their influence at the polls, guys like Joe the Plumber aren't typically campaign contributors. You're more likely to see John the Bond Trader bankrolling these campaigns."

About the Center for Responsive Politics
Celebrating its 25th year in 2008, the Center for Responsive Politics is the nation's premier research group

tracking money in US politics and its effect on elections and public policy. The nonpartisan, nonprofit Center aims to create a more educated voter, an involved citizenry and a more responsive government. CRP's award-winning website, OpenSecrets.org, is the most comprehensive resource for campaign contributions, lobbying data and analysis available anywhere.

For other organizations and news media, CRP's exclusive data powers their online features tracking money in politics. CRP relies on support from a combination of foundation grants and individual contributions. The Center accepts no contributions from businesses, labor unions or trade associations.

ON HEALTH

Now that we have covered election spending, let's move on to health in America.

How does a nation that prides itself on physical fitness with a fanatical obsession on sport, from peewee to high school to the pros, get to be this overweight?

Did you know that in the 1950s, professional football linemen averaged six feet two inches tall and weighed an average of 234 pounds? In 2011, that number was six feet five inches and 310 pounds. My friends, even some of your sports heroes are supersized.

And then, how about fast foods and poor nutrition? And what about the cost this is placing and will continue to be placing on your troubled health-care system and your general well-being for generations to come?

CHART OUTLINING OBESITY RATES

Country	Organization for Economic Cooperation and Development (OECD) 2012 Percentage of Population Fifteen Years of Age and Over Classified as Obese
United States	35.3
Canada	25.4
Japan	3.6
Czech Republic	21
Norway	10
Sweden	11.8
United Kingdom	24.7
Italy	10.4
Spain	16.6
France	14.5
Germany	14.7
Australia	28.3
New Zealand	31.3

GRAPH OUTLINING OBESITY RATES

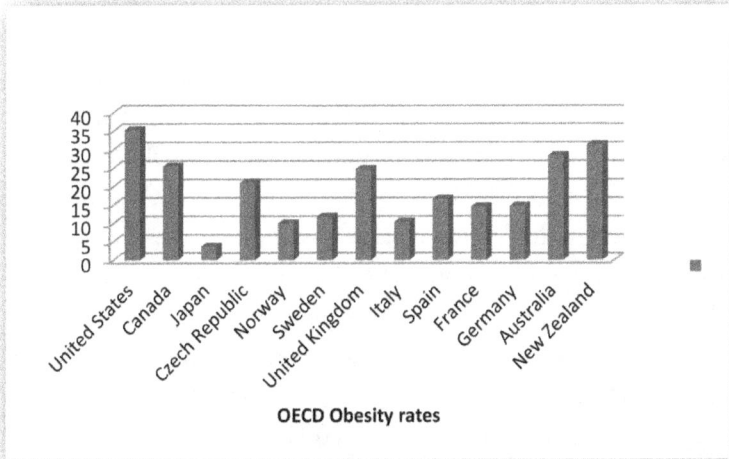

OECD Obesity rates

Your health-care system (if you want to call it that) is broken, and the will to look after your people is missing in Washington. If this health-care-building process had started years ago as Social Security did (and, incidentally, as we did in Canada over fifty years ago), you would not be in the mess you are in today. Lobbyists from both the insurance companies and the pharmaceutical industry have been major contributors to the problem.

People died in Arizona in 2010 because there were no funds for transplants.

Really! In these United States of America!

Families have been wiped out financially because of medical bills.

Really! In the good old US of A?

Oh, but wait! Have you checked the balance sheets of the pharmaceutical and insurance companies who run your health-care system and Wall Street, which funds them? How about the balance sheets of the lobbyists who do their bidding in Washington?

As an example, United Health Group, the largest health-care provider in America reported net income for 2015 of over $5.8 billion with net assets of over $33 billion.

Health Care for America Now reported that the top eleven pharmaceutical companies reported profits in 2012 of almost $84 billion, a 62 percent increase from 2003.

And as far as the lobbyists are concerned, what would Washington be without them? How about a more productive and honest town, as your elected officials would not be kowtowing to them at election time. Just my opinion, mind you!

And you should be thrilled but not surprised by the following. *Huffington Post* reported that the single largest cause for personal bankruptcy in America is medical bills.[11]

And maybe a violent and unhealthy society make for an unsustainable health care system.

---

11 http://www.huffingtonpost.com/simple-thrifty-living/top-10-reasons-people-go-_b_6887642.html

ON POVERTY

How does such a wealthy nation permit itself to have such a high poverty rate in this day and age? How about wealth inequality, where the rich have so much, the poor so little, and the middle class is heading south to join them?

The USDA has been running the SNAP (Supplemental Nutrition Program) for many years. Here are some numbers for you to think about.

* In 1969, there were 2,878,000 people receiving assistance at a cost of $250,000.000.
* In 1990, there were 20,949,000 people receiving assistance at a cost of $15,447,000,000.
* In 2014, there were 46,664,000 people receiving assistance at a cost of $74,162,160,000.

Considering this, you could be worse in the following chart listing. But don't rest on your laurels. After all, you are the best country in the world! Wake up, America; you can do better!

CHART OUTLINING THE DETAILS OF POVERTY RATES
(CIA, *World Fact Book*)

Percentage of Population below Poverty Line	Rate	Year
United States	15.1	2010
Canada	9.4	2008
Japan	16.1	2013
Czech Republic	8.6	2012
Norway	4.3	2007
Sweden	14.1	2011
United Kingdom	15	2013
Italy	19.6	2011
Spain	21.1	2012
France	8.1	2012
Germany	15.5	2010
Australia	13.9	2012*
New Zealand	n/a	n/a

* Australian numbers not from study but from direct research. New Zealand not reported at all.

GRAPH OUTLINING THE DETAILS OF POVERTY RATES

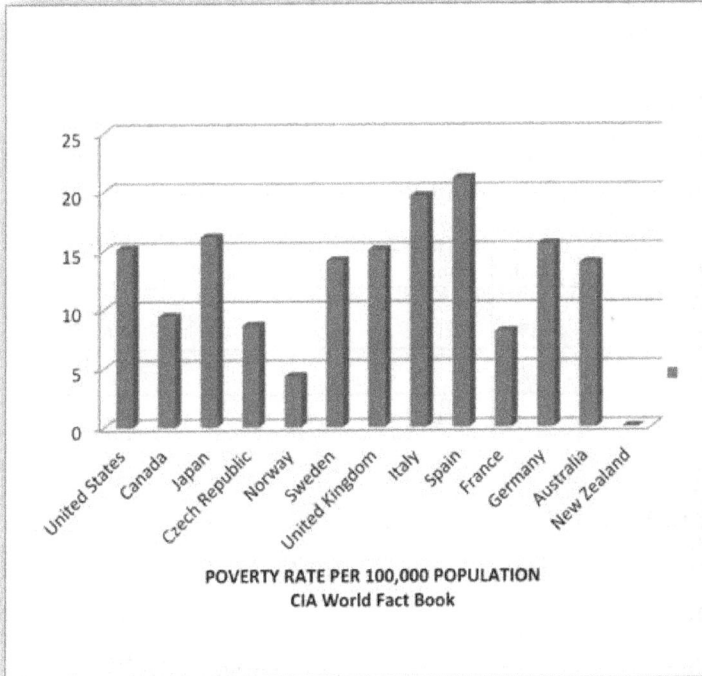

POVERTY RATE PER 100,000 POPULATION
CIA World Fact Book

EDUCATION

How does a country and its people with such potential and re-
sources end up ranking thirty-sixth, twenty-eighth, and twenty-
fifth in this PISA study? I don't have the answer, but you had
better come up with one soon. You can't keep importing brain-
power from overseas forever. You actually spend similar amounts
per capita as most of our study nations.

In 2015 and according to the *Hartford Courant*, Uconn men's basketball team graduation rate was only 22%.

Only 12 of 64 teams in the 2017 NCAA men's basketball tournament graduated 100% of it's players.

CHART OUTLINING THE DETAILS OF EDUCATION STANDINGS
(OECD/PISA Education Report 2012)

Country	Math	Rank	Science	Rank	Reading	Rank
Mean score	494		501		496	
USA	481	36	497	28	496	25
Canada	518	13	525	10	523	7
Japan	536	7	547	4	538	4
Czech Rep.	494	24	508	22	493	26
Norway	489	30	495	31	504	22
Sweden	478	38	485	38	483	36
UK	494	26	514	20	499	23
Italy	485	32	494	32	490	27
Spain	484	33	496	29	488	30
France	495	25	499	26	505	21
Germany	514	16	524	12	508	19
Australia	504	19	521	16	512	13
New Zealand	500	22	516	18	512	13

GRAPH OUTLINING THE DETAILS OF EDUCATION

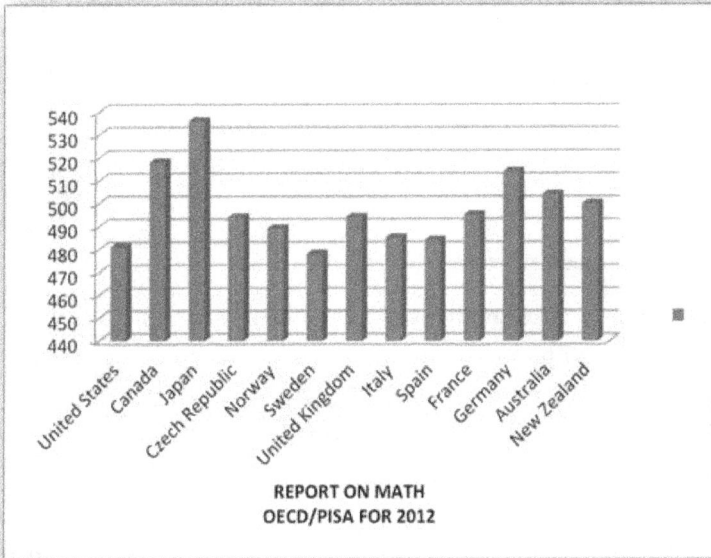

REPORT ON MATH
OECD/PISA FOR 2012

ON DRUGS IN AMERICA

What do gun violence, broken families, poverty, high medical bills, and death have in common? America's drug problem, that's what!

Actually, it's not only America's problem because you have exported it to my country directly, and you are destroying the entire fabric of your neighbors to the south. Drug wars in Mexico and Latin America are killing thousands of innocent people, and those who survive have no place to go.

Ah, yes, they do! They sneak across the border to America for a better life. If you will deal with America's drug problems, I will wager that most Mexican and Latin American people would gladly stay home!

There! I may be wrong, but I may have just fixed the majority of your immigration problem—and Donald Trump won't have to have Mexico build his wall.

⁂

Until you declare America's drug problem a national health crisis, there is no hope for a positive resolution to this horrendous, country-destroying problem.

And here is the latest. While America claims less than 5% of the world's population, it consumes roughly 80% of the world's opioid supply.[12]

Be careful how you read the following chart. Being ranked third in this study is not a good sign.

---

12   A NATION IN PAIN AN EXPRESS SCRIPTS REPORT | DECEMBER 2014. Manchikanti L, Singh A. Therapeutic opioids: a ten-year perspective on the complexities and complications of escalating use, abuse, and nonmedical use of opioids. Pain Physician. 2008;11(2 Suppl):S63-S88.

CHART OUTLINING THE RATE OF DRUG DEATHS

World Health Organization 2014 worldlifeexpectancy.com	Rate per 100,000 population	Rank
United States	6.96	3
Canada	2.29	49
Japan	0.43	127
Czech Republic	0.4	131
Norway	3.96	16
Sweden	2.49	40
United Kingdom	3.83	19
Italy	1.07	88
Spain	0.93	93
France	1.08	87
Germany	1.34	76
Australia	3.32	28
New Zealand	2.39	46

GRAPH OUTLINING THE RATE OF DRUG DEATHS

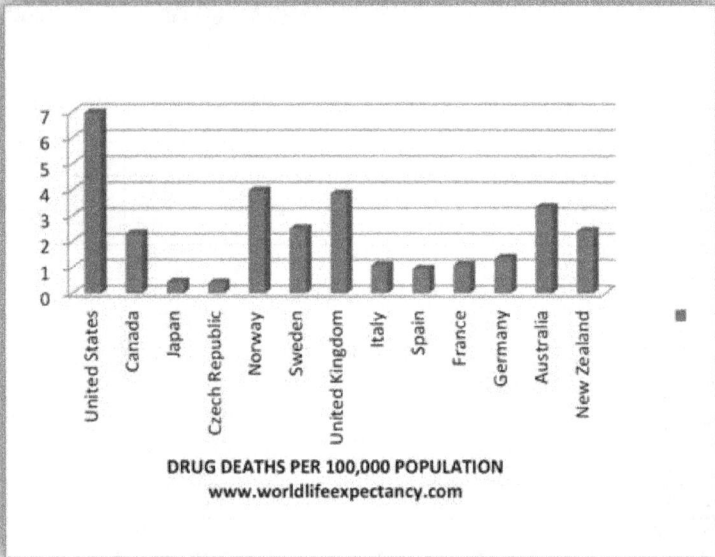

DRUG DEATHS PER 100,000 POPULATION
www.worldlifeexpectancy.com

ON DRUNK DRIVING IN AMERICA

* Every day in America, another twenty-eight people die as a result of drunk-driving crashes.[13]
* The average drunk driver has driven drunk eighty times before his or her first arrest.[14]

---

13 National Highway Traffic Safety Administration FARS data, 2014, http://www-nrd.nhtsa.dot.gov/Pubs/812102.pdf

14 Centers for Disease Control. "Vital Signs: Alcohol-Impaired Driving among Adults—United States, 2010," *Morbidity and Mortality Weekly Report*, October 4, 2011.

* Every two minutes, a person is injured in a drunk-driving crash.[15]
* Drunk driving costs the United States $199 billion a year.[16]
* On average, two in three people will be involved in a drunk-driving crash in their lifetime.[17]

---

15 National Highway Traffic Safety Administration, "The Economic and Societal Impact of Motor Vehicle Crashes, 2010," National Highway Traffic Safety Administration, May 2014, DOT HS 812 013, http://www-nrd.nhtsa.dot.gov/Pubs/812013.pdf.

16 National Highway Traffic Safety Administration, "The Economic and Societal Impact of Motor Vehicle Crashes, 2010," National Highway Traffic Safety Administration, May 2014, DOT HS 812 013, http://www-nrd.nhtsa.dot.gov/Pubs/812013.pdf.

17 National Highway Traffic Safety Administration, "The Economic and Societal Impact of Motor Vehicle Crashes, 2010," National Highway Traffic Safety Administration, May 2014, DOT HS 812 013, http://www-nrd.nhtsa.dot.gov/Pubs/812013.pdf.

CHALLENGE

My friends, pick any of the examples in this chapter and this is how America and Americans have been perceived for far too long a time, whether you like it or not or admit it or not or care about it or not.

Isn't it time, that you make an effort as a country and citizens to make the changes you need to, in order to become what you were meant to be as a country and as a people?

Doesn't the next generation and the one after that deserve to be viewed in a much better light?

Doesn't your country deserve to be called *"a kinder and gentler nation,"* as President George H.W. Bush alluded to, within the next generation?

So call, write, or e-mail your politicians. Get together as a neighborhood and see what you can do as a community. Above all, don't give up—move forward. Go to your own social media accounts and let other Americans know how you are feeling about America and especially what *you* are doing about these issues.

Consider yourselves challenged and encouraged!

Chapter 5

FROM MUSKETS TO WINCHESTERS TO AK-47S

To many, this may be the most contentious chapter of the book. Your famous or infamous Second Amendment to the Constitution (as you well know) reads, "A well regulated Militia, being necessary to the security of a free State, the right of the people to keep and bear Arms, shall not be infringed."

Dare I say that more Americans probably know these words better than the Lord's Prayer!

Did you know that your Constitution has been amended twenty-seven times since 1787; the last time being 1992? I guess changes can be made with the proper will of the people.

Now, the Declaration of Independence, which precedes the Constitution by some eleven years, was signed on July 4, 1776, by *unanimous* consent of all thirteen states.

The second paragraph of that amazing document reads, "We hold these truths to be self-evident, that all men are created equal, that they are endowed by their Creator with certain unalienable Rights that among these are Life, Liberty and the pursuit of Happiness."

The part that sticks out so clearly for me in those precious words is the right of life.

My friends, the time has come for America to choose between the two of them: the right to bear arms or the right to life. In 2016 and beyond, you cannot have both.

America has gone from the "Wild, Wild West," to the wild, wild, north, east and south as well.

Relax! No one is going to take away your guns! Sadly.

In my country, we are all able to own hunting rifles and have some of the best hunting in the world; ask your fellow hunters. But who needs AK-47s to shoot a deer? And who needs thirteen handguns to protect themselves?

As of 2015, there are 322 million people in America, and you are the proud owners of over 310 million firearms. That's got to make you proud, doesn't it? Yet does this make sense to anyone at all? You wait long enough (and it won't be long), and there will be one gun for each of you. And you can all get together and sing "Kumbaya."

I know the passing of good gun laws will not put an end to gun violence, but it will surely diminish it—just like putting highway dividers at dangerous places along the roadways did not stop all car deaths, just like the passing of seat-belt laws did not protect every person in a car accident, just like the smart states that passed laws that require motorcycle helmets did not prevent all motorcycle deaths.

But what if the passing of good, strong gun laws would save the life of that next little girl sitting on her stoop in Chicago? Would that be worthwhile?

Or the life of that three-year-old who was shot by her six-year-old sibling because her dad left the handgun unsecured?

Or the life of that four-year-old who was killed recently in a road-rage incident?

Or that of the nine-year-old who was lured into an alley by a gang member and shot to death in retaliation for his father's actions?

In fact, in Chicago, in recent high-school graduation ceremonies, they take the time to pause and read the names of those students who have been killed that year? Really?

⚔

But let's pause for a moment, shall we, and have a look at that lame mental-health excuse that is thrown out there by the NRA and gun advocates. Here is my question: Could passing strong and effective gun-control laws not happen quicker than dealing with the mental-health issues?

Oh, wait! Not in this session of Congress and not with the present mind-set of the infamous NRA and its supporters. I hear commentators and the NRA all the time, and so do you, saying it is not about guns but about mental health. Really! That's the best they have?

Well, that's good, because that means that Canada and many other countries listed in our charts must have much fewer mental-health problems.

As I write this chapter in October 2015, a five-month-old and a nine-month-old were killed in drive-by shootings. Where is the mental-health issue in that? How about just evil? How about an entire society on the edge of destruction?

I am going to take you through some statistics, historical information, and events that I hope you will think about and maybe even consider doing something about.

Here's an interesting number for you to start with. Over a recent two-year period, more people have been killed by firearms on the streets of America than there were soldiers killed in the jungles of Vietnam. Over 58,000 soldiers gave their lives.[18]

Here are a few more from the Brady Campaign sourced through CDC.

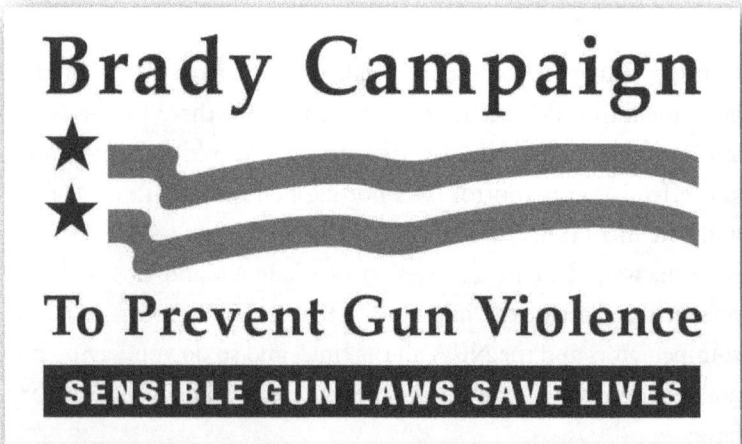

In one year's average between 2009 and 2013, the following happened:

---

18   http://www.thewall-usa.com/summary.asp.

31,224 people died from gun violence.

12,632 people were murdered.

2,161 children and teens were murdered.

3,067 children and teens died in gun-related events.

683 children and teens killed themselves.

351 people were killed by police intervention.

17,352 people committed suicide.

613 were killed accidentally.

Source: The Brady Campaign averaged the most recent five years of complete data (2009–2013) from death certificates and estimates from emergency-room admissions available via CDC's National Center for Injury Prevention and Controls Web-Based Injury Statistics Query and Reporting System, www.cdc.gov/ncipc/wisgars. Data retrieved 1.22.15.

CHART OUTLINING THE DETAILS OF MURDER RATES FOR 2012

Country	Rate per 100,000	Total
United States	4.7	14827
Canada	1.6	543
Japan	0.3	442
Czech Republic	1	105
Norway	2.2	111
Sweden	0.7	68
United Kingdom	1	653
Italy	0.9	530
Spain	0.8	364
France	1	655
Germany	0.8	662
Australia	1.1	254
New Zealand	0.9	41

United Nations Office on Drugs and Crime (UNODC) Murder Rates 2012

GRAPH OUTLINING THE
DETAILS OF MURDER RATES

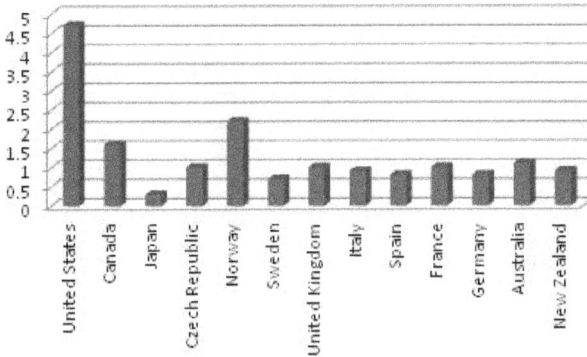

MURDER RATES PER 100,000 POPULATION
United Nations Office on Drugs and Crime 2012 Report

CHART OUTLINING THE DETAILS OF MURDER RATES BY FIREARM

Country	Rate per 100,000	Year
United States	5.3	2011
Canada	1.36	2012
Japan	0.8	2012
Czech Republic	1.75	2012
Norway	0.3	2010
Sweden	0.85	2011
United Kingdom	1.03	2011
Italy	0.89	2012
Spain	0.2	2011
France	0.06	2011
Germany	0.8	2011
Australia	1.1	2011
New Zealand	0.97	2010

World Health Organization (2012)

GRAPH OUTLINING THE DETAILS OF MURDER RATES BY FIREARM

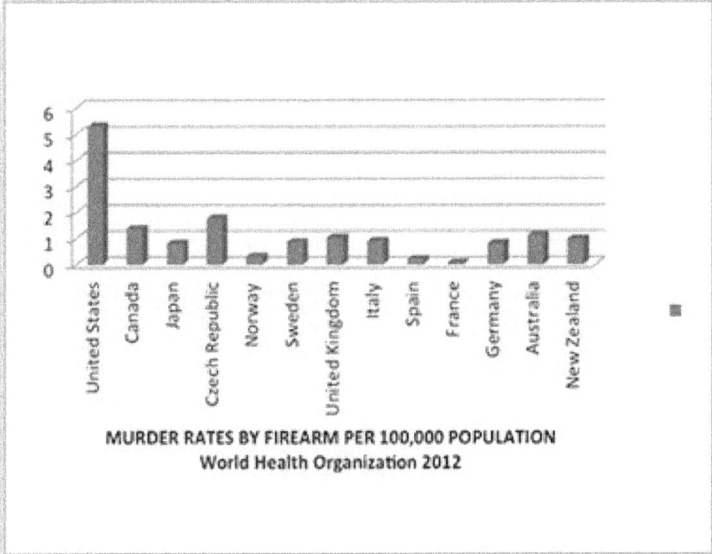

MURDER RATES BY FIREARM PER 100,000 POPULATION
World Health Organization 2012

CHART OUTLINING THE DETAILS OF SUICIDES BY FIREARM, RATE PER 100,000

	By Firearm	Total	Year
Rate per 100,000 Population			
United States	6.7	12.1	2012
Canada	1.6	9.8	2007–11
Japan	0.04	18.5	1999
Czech Republic	1.39	12.5	2010
Norway	1.72	9.28	2010
Sweden	1.2	11.1	2010
United Kingdom	0.17	6.28	2010
Italy	0.81	4.76	2009
Spain	0.42	5.1	2010
France	2.33	12.3	2009
Germany	0.94	9.2	2010
Australia	0.62	10.65	2011
New Zealand	1.14	9.6	2007

World Health Organization (2012)

GRAPH OUTLINING THE DETAILS OF SUICIDES

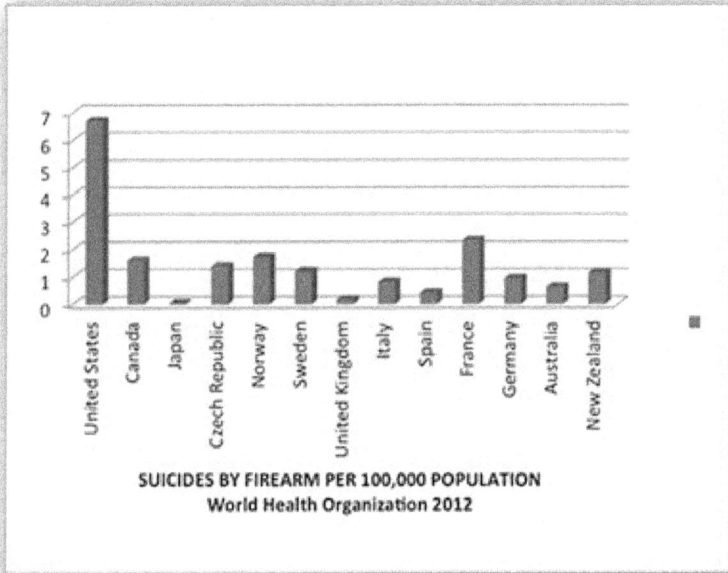

SUICIDES BY FIREARM PER 100,000 POPULATION
World Health Organization 2012

CHART OUTLINING INCARCERATION RATES

Country	Number of Prisoners per 100,000 Population
United States	707
Canada	118
Japan	51
Czech Republic	163
Norway	72
Sweden	60
United Kingdom	148
Italy	100
Spain	144
France	103
Germany	78
Australia	143
New Zealand	183

From the International Centre for Prison Studies (2014).

GRAPH OUTLINING
INCARCERATION RATES

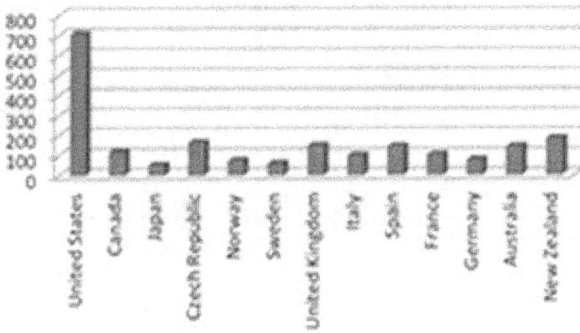

INCARCERATION RATES PER 100,000 POPULATION
International Centre for Prison Studies 2014

CHART OUTLINING THE DETAILS OF RAPE CRIMES, RATE PER 100,000

Report on Rape	Total	Rate	Year
Rate per 100,000 Population			
United States	84,767	27.3	2010
Canada	576	1.7	2010
Japan	1289	1	2010
Czech Republic	480	4.6	2009
Norway	938	19.2	2010
Sweden	2261	25.2	2004
United Kingdom	884	17	2009
Italy	4513	7.6	2006
Spain	1578	3.4	2010
France	10108	16.2	2009
Germany	7724	9.4	2010
Australia	10.65	0.62	2011
New Zealand	9.6	1.14	2007

From the United Nations Office on Drug and Crime.

GRAPH OUTLINING THE DETAILS OF RAPE CRIMES

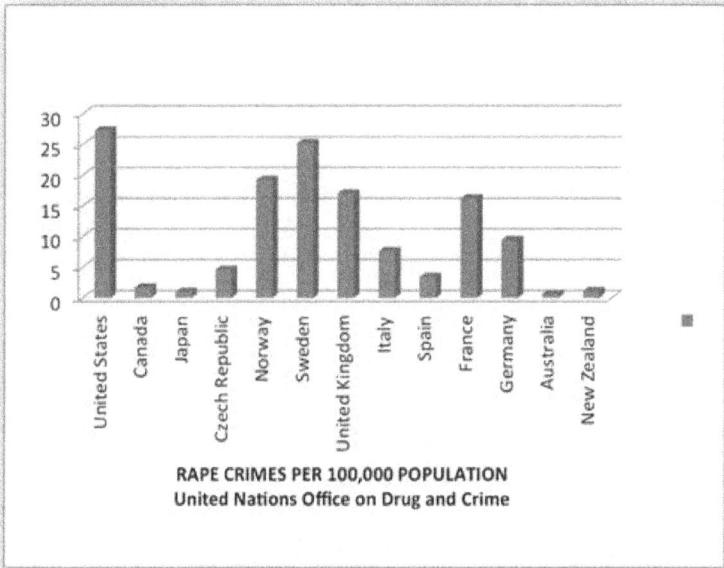

RAPE CRIMES PER 100,000 POPULATION
United Nations Office on Drug and Crime

And here are just a few of America's evilest people. Some of these you may remember, and some you won't, but all are a part of your violent past.

Richard Speck	Richard Dahmer	George Henard
Fort Hood shooter	Gail Halverson	James Huberty
Ted Bundy	BTK Shooter	Antares Wong
Unabomber	Howard Unruh	Newtown shooter
Joe Stack	Lee Harvey Oswald	James Pough

John Wilkes Booth

Son of Sam

David Koresh

Clarence Bertucci

Aurora, CO, shooter

William Jones

Robert Stewart

Nicholas Shelly

Larry Ashbrook

Aaron Huff

Atlanta church shooter

Washington, DC, Snipers

Charles Manson

Jim Jones

Andrea Yates

Aileen Wuornos

Luigi Ferri

Robert Hawkins

Ken Wayne

Monroe Phillips

Roland Smith

William Cornell

Michael McLendon

Charles Starkweather

Gilbert Twigg

Michael Silka

Walter Jones

Robert Brown

Scott Dekraai

Robert Charles

Jared Loughner

Columbine shooters

And there are too many more incidences of gun violence involving more than one victim since 1906 to list.

SOME OF THE MURDERS INCLUDING AND SINCE COLUMBINE IN 1999

(The names of the shooters have been omitted here and above, as I don't want to give them any more notoriety than they already have.)

April 1999—Two teenage schoolboys shot and killed twelve schoolmates and a teacher at Columbine High School in Littleton, Colorado, before killing themselves.

July 1999—A stock-exchange trader in Atlanta, Georgia, killed twelve people, including his wife and two children before taking his own life.

September 1999—A gunman opened fire at a prayer service in Fort Worth, Texas, killing six people before committing suicide.

October 2002—A series of sniper-style shootings occurred in Washington, DC, leaving ten dead.

August 2003—In Chicago, a laid-off worker shot and killed six of his former workmates.

November 2004—In Birchwood, Wisconsin, a hunter killed six other hunters and wounded two more after having an argument with them.

March 2005—A man opened fire at a church service in Brookfield, Wisconsin, killing seven people.

October 2006—A truck driver killed five schoolgirls and seriously wounded six others in a school in Nickel Mines, Pennsylvania, before taking his own life.

April 2007—A student shot and killed thirty-two people and wounded fifteen others at Virginia Tech in Blacksburg, Virginia, before shooting himself, making it the deadliest mass shooting in the United States after 2000.

August 2007—Three Delaware State University students were shot and killed in "execution style" by a twenty-eight-year-old and two fifteen-year-old boys. A fourth student was shot and stabbed.

December 2007—A twenty-year-old man killed nine people and injured five others in a shopping center in Omaha, Nebraska.

December 2007—A woman and her boyfriend shot dead six members of her family on Christmas Eve in Carnation, Washington.

February 2008—A shooter (who is still at large) tied up and shot six women at a suburban clothing store in Chicago, leaving five of them dead and the remaining one injured.

February 2008—A man opened fire in a lecture hall at Northern Illinois University in DeKalb, Illinois, killing five students and wounding sixteen others before laying down his weapon and surrendering.

July 2008—A former student shot three people in a computer lab at South Mountain Community College, Phoenix, Arizona.

September 2008—A mentally ill man, who had been released from jail one month earlier, shot eight people in Alger, Washington, leaving six of them dead and two wounded.

October 2008—Several men in a car drove up to a dormitory at the University of Central Arkansas and opened fire, killing two students and injuring a third person.

December 2008—A man dressed in a Santa Claus suit opened fire at a family Christmas party in Covina, California, and then set fire to the house and killed himself. Police later found nine people dead in the debris of the house.

March 2009—A twenty-eight-year-old laid-off worker opened fire while driving a car through several towns in Alabama, killing ten people.

March 2009—A heavily armed gunman shot dead eight people, many of them elderly and sick people, in a private-owned nursing home in North Carolina.

March 2009—Six people were shot dead in a high-grade apartment building in Santa Clara, California.

April 2009—An eighteen-year-old former student followed a pizza-delivery man into his old dormitory and then shot the deliveryman, a dorm monitor, and himself at Hampton University, Virginia.

April 2009—A man shot dead thirteen people at a civic center in Binghamton, New York.

July 2009—Six people, including one student, were shot in a drive-by shooting at a community rally on the campus of Texas Southern University, Houston.

November 2009—A US Army psychologist opened fire at a military base in Fort Hood, Texas, leaving thirteen dead and forty-two others wounded.

February 2010—A professor opened fire fifty minutes into a biological-sciences department faculty meeting at the University of Alabama, killing three colleagues and wounding three others.

January 2011—A gunman opened fire at a public gathering outside a grocery store in Tucson, Arizona, killing six people (including a nine-year-old girl) and wounding at least twelve others. Congresswoman Gabrielle Giffords was severely injured with a gunshot to the head.

July 2012—A masked gunman opened fire at a midnight cinema screening of the film The Dark Knight Rises, killing twelve and injuring fifty-eight.

August 2012—A gunman killed six people at Sikh temple in Wisconsin before being shot dead by police. The suspect was named as white supremacist.

December 2012—A young man forced his way into Sandy Hook Elementary School in Newtown, Connecticut. He killed twenty first graders and six adults. Before arriving at the school, he had killed his mother at their home.

June 2013—An unemployed twenty-three-year-old man killed five people in a rampage that began at his father's home and ended in Santa Monica College's library.

September 2013—A navy contractor and former navy man engaged police in a running firefight in a Washington, DC, industrial complex before being shot and killed. Thirteen people were killed and three injured.

May 2014—A man opened fire in the campus town of Isla Vista, California, from inside a black BMW, killing seven people. He acted alone, and written and video evidence suggest the attack was premeditated.

June 2015—White supremacist began shooting in a historic black church in an attempt to start a race war. He killed nine people.

August 2015—A man shot dead two former colleagues from the WDBJ7 news team.

October 2015—A young man went into Umpqua Community College in Roseburg, Oregon, and killed nine people and injured nine more. He owned fourteen firearms.

December 2015—A man and a woman entered a Christmas party in a government building in San Bernardino, California, and killed fourteen people and injured seventeen more. They were killed a few hours later in a police shootout. [19]

Another day 2015—where and by whom and who are the next victims?

Next shooting-
Next shooting-
First mass shooting 2016…

And then there was Orlando!

And then there was Dallas!

And nothing has yet been done even after twenty children and six adults were killed in Sandy Hook School. Really? In these United States of America!

And the violence in America has not spared your leaders, either…

PRESIDENTS ASSASSINATED BY AMERICANS

ABRAHAM LINCOLN

On Friday, April 14, 1865, at approximately 10:15 p.m., Lincoln was shot once in the back of his head with a .44-caliber Derringer pistol by actor and Confederate sympathizer John Wilkes Booth while the president was watching the play *Our American Cousin* at Ford's Theatre in Washington, DC.

---

19 http://www.telegraph.co.uk/news/worldnews/northamerica/usa/9414540/A-history-of-mass-shootings-in-the-US-since-Columbine.html

He remained in a coma for nine hours before dying the following morning at 7:22 a.m. on April 15. Booth was tracked down by Union soldiers, and he was shot and killed by Sergeant Boston Corbett on April 26, 1865.

JAMES A. GARFIELD

On Saturday, July 2, 1881, fewer than four months after the president took office, Charles J. Guiteau shot President Garfield twice.

Garfield died eleven weeks later, on September 19, 1881, at 10:35 p.m., of complications caused by infections. Guiteau was immediately arrested, and after a highly publicized trial that lasted from November 14, 1881, to January 25, 1882, he was found guilty, sentenced to death, and finally executed by hanging on June 30, 1882.

WILLIAM MCKINLEY

On Friday, September 6, 1901, President McKinley was shot twice in the abdomen at close range by Leon Czolgosz, a self-proclaimed anarchist.

McKinley died eight days later, on September 14, 1901. On September 24, after a rushed, two-day trial in federal court, Czolgosz was sentenced to death. He was executed by electric chair in Auburn Prison on October 29, 1901.

JOHN F. KENNEDY

On Friday, November 22, 1963, in Dallas, Texas, Kennedy was fatally wounded by Lee Harvey Oswald, who shot at and hit him twice, while the president was riding with his wife, Jacqueline, in a presidential motorcade through Dealey Plaza. Lee Harvey Oswald was arrested shortly after at the Texas Theater.

At 11:21 a.m., Sunday, November 24, 1963, while he was handcuffed to Detective Jim Leavelle and about to be taken to the Dallas County Jail, Oswald was shot and fatally wounded in the basement of Dallas Police Headquarters by Jack Ruby, a Dallas nightclub operator.

Oswald was taken unconscious by ambulance to Parkland Memorial Hospital where he died at 1:07 p.m.

ASSASSINATION ATTEMPTS OR PLOTS ON PRESIDENTS BY AMERICANS

ANDREW JACKSON

On January 30, 1835, just outside the Capitol building, a house painter named Richard Lawrence attempted to shoot Jackson with two separate pistols, both of which misfired.

Lawrence was apprehended after Jackson beat him severely with his cane. Lawrence was found not guilty by reason of insanity and confined to a mental institution until his death in 1861.

ABRAHAM LINCOLN

On February 23, 1861, an alleged conspiracy to assassinate President-elect Abraham Lincoln en route to his inauguration, called the Baltimore Plot, occurred. Allan Pinkerton, founder of the Pinkerton National Detective Agency, played a key role in protecting the president-elect by managing Lincoln's security throughout the journey. Though scholars debate whether or not the threat was real, Lincoln and his advisers took actions to ensure his safe passage through Baltimore.

In August 1864, a lone rifle shot missed Lincoln's head by inches (passing through his hat) as he rode in the late evening, unguarded, north from the White House three miles to Soldiers' Home (his regular retreat where he would work and sleep before returning to the White House the following morning). Near eleven o'clock in the evening, Private John W. Nichols, the sentry on duty at the gated entrance, heard the rifle shot and moments later saw the president riding toward him bareheaded.

WILLIAM HOWARD TAFT
In October 1909, Taft was at a summit in El Paso, Texas, and Ciudad Juárez, Mexico. This was a historic first meeting between a US president and a Mexican president and also the first time an American president would cross the border into Mexico.

On October 16, the day of the summit, a Texas Ranger discovered a man holding a concealed palm pistol, standing at the El Paso Chamber of Commerce building along the procession route. The would-be assassin was arrested within only a few feet of Taft and Mexican president Díaz.

THEODORE ROOSEVELT
On October 14, 1912, three and a half years after he left office, Roosevelt was running for president as a member of the Progressive Party. John F. Schrank, a saloon keeper from New York who had been stalking him for weeks, shot Roosevelt once in the chest. Schrank was immediately disarmed, captured, and might have been lynched had Roosevelt not shouted for him to remain unharmed. After discerning he was not mortally wounded, Roosevelt finished his speech with the bullet still lodged in his chest.

Afterward, he went to a nearby hospital, where the bullet was found between his ribs. Doctors decided it would be too risky to remove it, so the bullet remained in Roosevelt's body for the rest of his life. He spent two weeks recuperating before returning to the campaign trail. Despite his tenacity, Roosevelt ultimately lost his bid for reelection.

FRANKLIN D. ROOSEVELT
On February 15, 1933, in Miami, Florida, Giuseppe Zangara fired five shots at Roosevelt. Although the president-elect was not hurt, four other people were wounded, and Chicago Mayor Anton Cermak was killed. Zangara was found guilty of murder and was executed March 20, 1933.

HARRY S. TRUMAN
On November 1, 1950, two Puerto Rican pro-independence activists, Oscar Collazo and Griselio Torresola, attempted to kill Truman at the Blair House, where Truman lived while the White House was being renovated. In the attack, Torresola mortally wounded White House Policeman Leslie Coffelt, who killed the attacker. Truman was not harmed but was at risk. He commuted Collazo's death sentence, after conviction in a federal trial, to life in prison. In 1979, President Jimmy Carter commuted it to time served.

JOHN F. KENNEDY
On December 11, 1960, while vacationing in Palm Beach, Florida, President-elect John F. Kennedy was threatened by Richard Paul Pavlick. Pavlick intended to crash his dynamite-laden 1950 Buick into Kennedy's vehicle, but he changed his mind after seeing Kennedy's wife

and daughter bid him good-bye. Pavlick was arrested three days later by the Secret Service. Pavlick spent the next six years in both federal prison and mental institutions before being released in December 1966.

RICHARD NIXON

On April 13, 1972, Arthur Bremer carried a firearm to an event intending to shoot Nixon, but he was put off by strong security. A few weeks later, he instead shot and seriously injured the governor of Alabama George Wallace.

On February 22, 1974, Samuel Byck planned to kill Nixon by crashing a commercial airliner into the White House. He hijacked the plane on the ground by force and was told that it could not take off with the wheel blocks still in place. After he shot the pilot and copilot, an officer shot Byck through the plane's door window. He survived long enough to kill himself by shooting.

GERALD FORD

On September 5, 1975, Lynette Fromme, a follower of Charles Manson, drew a pistol on Ford when he reached to shake her hand in a crowd. She had four cartridges in the pistol's magazine but none in the firing chamber, and as a result, the gun misfired. Fromme was sentenced to life in prison but was released from custody on August 14, 2009.

On September 22, 1975, in San Francisco, California, Sara Jane Moore fired a revolver at Ford from forty feet away. A bystander, Oliver Sipple, grabbed Moore's arm and the shot missed Ford. Moore was tried and convicted in federal court and sentenced to prison for life. She was paroled from a federal prison on December 31, 2007, after serving more than thirty years.

JIMMY CARTER

On May 5, 1979, in Los Angeles, Raymond Lee Harvey, an Ohio-born unemployed drifter, was arrested by the Secret Service after being found carrying a starter pistol with blank rounds ten minutes before Carter was to give a speech. Harvey had a history of mental illness, but police had to investigate his claim that he was part of a four-man operation to assassinate the president. Harvey was jailed on a $50,000 bond, given his transient status.

RONALD REAGAN

On March 30, 1981, in Washington, Reagan and three other men were shot and wounded by John Hinckley Jr. Reagan was struck by a single bullet, which broke a rib, punctured a lung, and caused serious internal bleeding. He was rushed to nearby George Washington University Hospital for emergency surgery and then hospitalized for about two weeks. John Hinckley Jr. was arrested, tried, and sentenced to life in prison, where he sits today.

BILL CLINTON

On January 21, 1994, Ronald Gene Barbour, a retired military officer and freelance writer, plotted to kill Clinton while the president was jogging. Barbour returned to Florida a week later without having fired the shots at the president. Barbour was sentenced to five years in prison and was released in 1998.

On September 12, 1994, Frank Eugene Corder flew a stolen single-engine Cessna onto the White House lawn and crashed into a tree, allegedly trying to hit the White House. He was killed in the crash. The president and first family were not home at the time.

On October 29, 1994, Francisco Martin Duran fired at least twenty-nine shots with a semiautomatic rifle at the White House from a fence overlooking the north lawn, thinking that Clinton was among the men in dark suits standing there. (Clinton was inside.) Three tourists tackled Duran before he could injure anyone. Found with a suicide note in his pocket, Duran was sentenced to forty years in prison.

BARACK OBAMA

In 2008, cousins Tharin Gartrell and Shawn Adolf and their friend Nathan Johnson went to Denver, allegedly planning to assassinate Obama during his acceptance speech at the 2008 Democratic National Convention, but officials said there was no substantial threat. The three men were arrested.

In 2008, a plot in Tennessee involved two white supremacists, Paul Schlesselman and Daniel Cowart, who planned to drive their car toward the Democratic nominee Obama and open fire with guns. They were arrested on October 22, 2008, before taking any action. Schlesselman and Cowart pleaded guilty to federal charges related to the threat in 2010 and were sentenced to ten and fourteen years in prison, respectively.

In November 2011, Oscar Ramiro Ortega-Hernandez, a man who believed that he was Jesus and that Obama was the Antichrist, hit the White House with several rounds fired from a semiautomatic rifle. No one was injured.

In April 2013, another attempt was made when a letter laced with ricin, a deadly poison, was sent to President Obama.

My friends, America is, by far, the most violent country in the free world, and I am not just talking about guns. Someone needs to take ownership of that, and everyone should be beyond embarrassed.

Is all your violence a case of life imitating art or art imitating life? Is the country so violent because of the violence in your TV programs, movies, and video games? Or are your TV programs, movies, and video games violent because of what is happening in your streets?

Is this not quite the story of the chicken and the egg?

C'mon, America! You can do better than this!

Your jails and prisons are full, and your people are afraid to walk the streets.

You drive through many communities and see steel-reinforced screened front doors bought at Home Depot.

Many sections of your cities are run by gangs, and your police departments are overwhelmed.

What might have become of that eight-year-old child killed on her stoop in Chicago? A teacher! A scientist! A president!

There is a lot at stake here, my friends, because that violence is being exported to my country of Canada and our neighbor Mexico—and much of that is related, as mentioned earlier, to the drug problem in America.

And fair warning here (and please don't write me later), as soon as the doors to Cuba open wide to Americans, that little country that has been sitting in the nineteen sixties for half a century will see an increase in violence, and those same open doors may be closed once again by Cuba sooner than we think.

⊰⊱

So what is it that makes your potentially great country so violent? That's the question you need to find the answer to!

Imagine the productivity increase if you could reduce that violence by 25 percent before the end of this decade; that impact would be palpable. Fewer people and families would be impacted. Fewer work days would be lost. You might even be able to begin rebuilding your inner cities. Imagine what the overall improved tone and spirit of the country would be like.

If you have read through this whole chapter and pondered the material, you are—I hope—experiencing a wide range of emotions. Sadly, that was one of my purposes! You must be somewhere between anger, frustration, embarrassment, disappointment, and sadness. What's to be done?

CHALLENGE

First of all, accept and face the reality of being the most violent country in the free world and stop thinking you are the greatest. It will be a tough thing for some to do, but it is so needed in order to move forward.

Then reach out to your circle and ask them to do the same. Have meetings with them and plan what you are going to do about the major issues this chapter outlines that are occurring in America today.

Don't let anyone tell you that nothing can be done, or else the premise of this book of a failed society will come to pass.

Stand up and take a stand where you need to, and get on your knees if people are not listening.

God may listen to you in your sincerity and ignore someone making a halfhearted comment asking for God's blessing!

Chapter 6

AND THE AWARD GOES TO...

Oscar Wilde opined the following in his 1889 essay, the "Decay of Lying," "Life imitates Art far more than art imitates life," and at this point in my life, I would wholeheartedly disagree. If art does not imitate life, then is it even art at all?

What does it say about a country that produces the kinds of programming listed in the following pages for its people? That free speech and freedom of expression that you hold on to so tightly is honorable—but at what cost? I have watched many of these programs and, if truth be told, have enjoyed parts of some of them—the characters that are portrayed, the visuals, and the slick production.

A single episode would probably not bother me at the time, but herein lies the rub. Package all of these together (many back to back) and drop yourself onto a couch for three to four hours or more, day in and day out, and just see if the effect is the same. Never mind the weight gain!

The realization that I came to was this: if all of the violence and sexual innuendo viewed could negatively affect a mature adult, what impact might it have on your young people and all of those unable to differentiate life from art or fact from fiction?

For the first time ever just a few months ago, I felt its noxious impact as I sat down and watched many of those programs consciously for the very last time. To me, this is not a constitutional affair dealing with freedoms. This is about the citizenry demanding the individual producers to deliver a better product that Americans had better want and need. They deliver the horrible products today for no other reason than the almighty dollar.

I do believe the artists and directors just might be satisfied and challenged enough if they were to be asked to do more empowering, caring, feel-good stories that would represent the best of America instead of the worst.

TV productions, like the ones you'll see listed on the next pages, have been seen by millions of your people. Could it be that there simply may not be enough feel-good, caring, or empowering stories in America for them to write a story about? Really?

From the outside looking in, this art form in its present state is not something to be proud of as a nation. The world sees this graphic violence and sexuality as America.

Is it?

Do you care what the world thinks about this?

Will it matter to your children?

I am a big fan of TV and honestly probably watch too much of it for my own good. There are truly some good programs that encourage and enlighten, but in recent years, I have been struck by the amount of violence that is prevalent today.

I am a simple guy and do not have a degree in psychology, but how can all of this violence *not* affect the American psyche, especially those who are experiencing any kind of emotional challenge?

Who is to blame? How about the people who watch the shows and those who produce them? Is this one of those chicken-and-egg deals where if they were not produced, they wouldn't be watched *or* they are produced because people want them? I'll let you decide.

Suffice to say that if the demand was not there, they would not get produced because there would be *no* money in it for the producers.

I do remember back in the day, and now I'm taking you back to the '50s, '60s, and '70s just for a moment. There were plenty of healthy family sitcoms and cop shows, where there was good humor and little or no bloodshed; somebody got shot and fell down, and that was it.

And guess what. People watched these shows, and producers and directors made them because that's what people wanted. Get it?

A couple of examples come to mind, and if you are of my vintage, you will happily remember more.

One was *Hawaii Five-0* where it was enjoyable to see the police get the bad guys without blood and body parts, where "Book 'em, Danno" was an end to a good story.

Another was the Dean Martin roasts that were actual family entertainment. Have you checked out today's versions? Well, don't! They are called celebrity roasts and are nothing but attempts at humor laced with profanity and sexual innuendo not fit for human consumption.

I guess they are deemed fit for human consumption, because some producer is making them, as there is money to be made.

But what does it say about those who participate in those shows? Think about that if you care to; it says a lot!

I would be remiss to leave this topic without commenting on what are arguably three of my favorite shows, two of which I have to say that I *used to* enjoy: the series *24*, the police documentary *First 48*, and the troubled teen program *Scared Straight*.

Let me share with you first about *24*. I made the mistake a few months ago of watching several episodes in a row and was blown away (pardon the pun) by the overwhelming heartsick feeling that came over me. If *I* got emotionally wired up from this, what about the borderline, now homegrown, terrorist sitting in his living room saying to himself, "I can do this" or "I could be one of them." Far out? I think not.

And now to the *First 48*. I was intrigued by this series because it was not fictional as most of the shows are today but real live documentaries of police and criminal activities in some of America's major cities. After watching most of one season, here is what I detected. The vast majority of criminals (over 75 percent) are either black or Latino. I understand full well that these are filmed in cities with high concentrations of these people groups, but what does it say about producers who package these?

It says that if there is an audience, there is money to be made, no matter what real or imagined perceptions are created about those people groups. I mentioned in an earlier chapter about what the people watching these shows might be thinking, whether they are white or black and Latino.

The *only* saving grace for me in the *First 48* series is the hard work police officers put into protecting their communities and bringing people to justice. But most of all, it is the feelings of sadness, frustration, and actual pain that I see on their faces when yet another needless and senseless crime occurs. How they keep doing what they do I do not know. All of you should be on your knees thanking your police departments every single day, regardless of the police violence issues facing America today. Those issues are very much there but, maybe, just maybe, if America was not so violent, you would need less law enforcement, and therefore, less of a chance for rogue or unfit police officers.

And finally, let's talk about *Scared Straight*. In this program, we get to view both sides of prison life from the young people's perspective. The first are the actual inmates who are serving various amounts of time and theoretically attempting to help out troubled teens by scaring them straight.

Then, you have these teens whose parents or the courts are trying to keep them out of jail; some of them have served time already.

And most, as the stories are told, come from broken homes. It saddens me so much to see troubled young people in so much pain only to have someone think that putting them on national television for all to see will be beneficial to them.

LET'S GO TO THE MOVIES... OR WE CAN JUST BRING A VIDEO GAME HOME?

What kind of society generates in its people a desire to see so many of the violent movies or video games that are produced in America today? For your viewing enjoyment, we have violent bad-guy ones, slashers, soft porn, and, for lack of a better word, the-dumbing-down-of-America movies and commercials.

And how are all of you enjoying your freedom of expression?
How is that working for you?

And, further, what impact are they having on young and old Americans alike?

What moral compass are the producers and studio owners working from that they would be proud of so many of these?

Does Quentin Tarantino, one of the premiere proponents of this genre, not care about the impact this stuff is having on America? Hang on, there; it's his right to make the movies he wants.

Folks! It's also his right and that of other like-minded producers, not to do them if they choose not to.

And then those same producers will say that there are few or no reliable scientific studies that relate violent movies with violence in America.

Now, I haven't checked—maybe someone could or has—but I bet you there are. In situations like this, the problem may be getting ten professional psychologists in a room and having them agree that there is or isn't. Good luck with that!

I have no degree on the matter, but what little common sense I have left after looking at this topic leads me to believe that there is a tremendous impact on people and it is showing up in your society.

In passing, I believe I heard in 2014, that one of Hollywood's most powerful producers was going to stop making violent movies. Bravo, Mr. Weinstein! I hope he has!

As I hinted at earlier, have you ever tried to sit down any night of the week to find a significant amount of good quality family viewing without violence?

How about the following peaceful viewing enjoyment this week on Arizona television?

NCIS	Miami Drug Cartel	Vegas Mafia
Blue Bloods	Gotham	Quantico
American Gothic	CSI	Castle
Romeo Section	Law and Order	Criminal Minds
Cops	Major Crimes	First 48
Empire	Chicago PD	48 Hours
Hawaii Five-0	The Blacklist	Bones
The Mentalist	Scandal	Person of Interest
Homicide Hunter	Lockup	Blindspot
The Walking Dead	How to Get Away with Murder	
Elementary	Rookie Blue	Rizzoli and Isles
Forensic Files	Blood & Oil	Code Black
Cops	Jail: Las Vegas	Outsiders
The Badlands	Ray Donovan	

And then don't forget the following life-enriching programs that are or have been on the small screen.

Maury Povich	Teen Mom	Honey Boo Boo
Toddlers and Tiaras	Love at First Swipe	Chrisley Know Best
Sex in Public	Steve Wilkos	Jerry Springer
Party Heat	Shake the Lake	Jersey Shore
Aquapallooza	Flavor Flav	Janice Dickinson
Rock of Love	Girls Gone Bad	
Vegas Confessions	Bikini Destinations	

And did I mention the character-building and values-setting presentations of these shows:

The Kardashian Empire	*General Hospital*
As the World Turns	*Young and the Restless*
One Life to Live	*The Bold and the Beautiful*
All My Children	*Desperate and Real Housewives*
Secretly Pregnant	*Married by Mom and Dad*

The production companies and studio owners need to be willing to lead in this area. They can be a very productive part of the upgraded moral fabric of your country.

Do they want to? Maybe!

Will they? Maybe!

When might they want to? When you stop viewing them!

Are you prepared to do something about it?

Isn't it time to ask for more great, uplifting programs like these from the past?

7th Heaven	*Marcus Welby*	*Lassie*
Family Ties	*Doogie Howser*	*Growing Pains*
Happy Days	*Little House on the Prairie*	*Bonanza*
The Waltons	*All in the Family*	*Brady Bunch*
Cheers	*Mash*	
Everybody Loves Raymond		

And a few more like these from present day...

Secret Millionaire	*Undercover Boss*	
Alaskan Bush People	*What Would You Do?*	
National Geographic	Hallmark Channel	
The Little Couple	*Dr. PolShark Tank*	*Little Big Shots*

Good luck finding some of these on the main networks, if you can find them at all. But I would bet that if enough of you were to ask for similar programming like back in the day, they would get made.

I also sincerely want to thank the CNN network for their production of the yearly series *CNN Heroes*, which depicts some amazing world heroes and, not surprisingly, many of them American.

⚎

Folks! Ask yourself this question. Why is it that as of December 1, when the Christmas TV season begins, it feels like the world is calmer and better?

Maybe, just maybe, it is because all the violent shows are on break, fewer people are watching the reruns, and the feel-good Christmas movies are on.

But then again, maybe that's just me—but I hope not!

CHALLENGE

Search on your own, get in touch with those producers we just talked about, and insist that they make more wholesome productions. Ask that they stop making poor productions with stories that simply do not meet the quality demanded of the new America. Let them know what you are feeling and what you are prepared to do.

Are you prepared to stop viewing them?

Are you prepared not to buy the products they peddle in the commercials?

Hold the producers and advertisers accountable. You don't need to go it alone; involve your family and friends in the process. Turn this into a petition to restore some semblance of values that were so much more prevalent just a few short decades ago.

Don't give up! Do it for future generations because, as in Washington, things will not happen quickly, but they will happen if you believe in your purpose and hang in there. You may want to see if one of your legislators has what it takes to tackle this one.

Folks, I believe those feel-good stories and heroes that I talked about earlier are out there, and I hope that those of you who read this book will be willing to share them with the rest of America.

Please share those stories with each other on social media to give anyone who needs one, a boost in their daily life. Maybe a producer will pick one up and make a great family movie.

As you are challenged to be *the* world leader, this would be an extremely important area to begin with. Remember that this art is viewed by children and adults around the world.

Chapter 7

IN GOD WE TRUST! REALLY?

"In God We Trust"
"God Bless America!"

You've got to be kidding!

I have heard the words "God bless the United States of America" and "God bless America" for as long as I can remember. I have heard them from every president and from your politicians and spoken as an afterthought or at the end of a speech that may or may not need a closing bit of emphasis.

I have heard "God Bless America" sung by Kate Smith at a Philadelphia Flyers hockey game, as part of the seventh-inning stretch at a baseball game, and at the great American pastime, a

NASCAR race. I have heard it sung at a Fourth of July celebration in Boston and at countless other venues.

But what does that request mean? Are those who utter those words still hoping for that blessing? I believe that is their fervent wish.

But what's missing? What's happened? Surely, America has not received God's blessing yet. For a country whose foundation was based on Judeo-Christian principles, look at where it is today.

The pages in this book have told part of the story as to why God has not answered. The God that I serve is not yet ready to bless a nation that has dropped so far away from what many believe it has been called to be and what your founding fathers had hoped for.

But first, a history lesson on "In God We Trust."

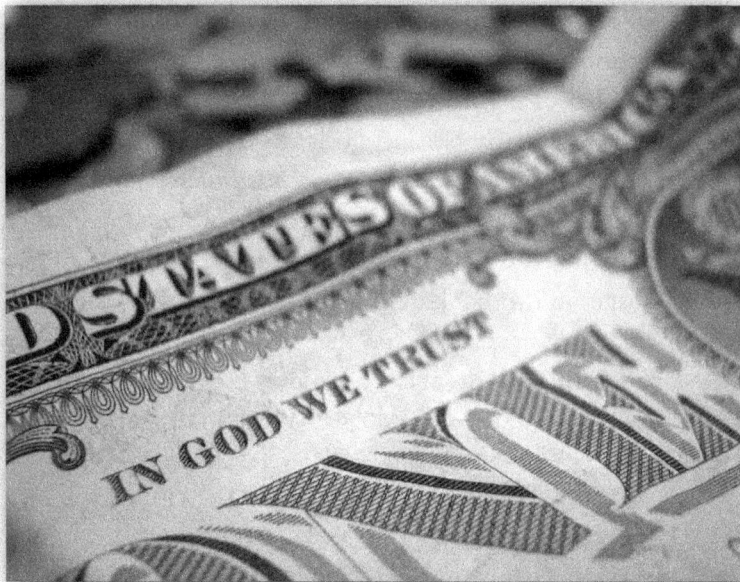

From Treasury Department records, it appears that the first suggestion that God be recognized on US coinage can be traced to a letter addressed to the Secretary of Treasury from a minister in 1861. An Act of Congress, approved on April 11, 1864, authorized the coinage of two-cent coins upon which the motto first appeared.

The motto was omitted from the new gold coins issued in 1907, causing a storm of public criticism. As a result, legislation passed in May 1908 made "In God We Trust" mandatory on all coins on which it had previously appeared.

Legislation approved July 11, 1955, made the appearance of "In God We Trust" mandatory on all coins and paper currency of the United States. By Act of July 30, 1956, "In God We Trust" became the national motto of the United States.

Several years ago, the appearance of "In God We Trust" on...money was challenged in the federal courts. The challenge was rejected by the lower federal courts, and the Supreme Court of the United States declined to review the case.[20]

The Department of Treasury reports the following:

The motto was placed on United States coins largely because of the increased religious sentiment existing during the Civil War. Secretary of the Treasury Salmon P. Chase received many appeals from devout persons throughout the country, urging that the United States recognize the Deity on United States coins. From Treasury Department records, it appears that the first such appeal came in a letter dated November 13, 1861. It was written to Secretary Chase by Rev. M. R. Watkinson, Minister of the Gospel from Ridleyville, Pennsylvania, and read:

Dear Sir:
You are about to submit your annual report to the Congress respecting the affairs of the national finances. One fact touching our currency has hitherto been seriously overlooked.

---

20 https://www.usmint.gov/about_the_mint/fun_facts/?action=fun_facts5.

I mean the recognition of the Almighty God in some form on our coins.

You are probably a Christian. What if our Republic were not shattered beyond reconstruction? Would not the antiquaries of succeeding centuries rightly reason from our past that we were a heathen nation? What I propose is that instead of the goddess of liberty we shall have next inside the 13 stars a ring inscribed with the words PERPETUAL UNION; within the ring the all seeing eye, crowned with a halo; beneath this eye the American flag, bearing in its field stars equal to the number of the States united; in the folds of the bars the words GOD, LIBERTY, LAW.

This would make a beautiful coin, to which no possible citizen could object. This would relieve us from the ignominy of heathenism. This would place us openly under the Divine protection we have personally claimed. From my heart I have felt our national shame in disowning God as not the least of our present national disasters.
To you first I address a subject that must be agitated.

As a result, Secretary Chase instructed James Pollock, Director of the Mint at Philadelphia, to prepare a motto, in a letter dated November 20, 1861:

Dear Sir: No nation can be strong except in the strength of God, or safe except in His defense. The trust of our people in God should be declared on our national coins. You will cause a device to be prepared without unnecessary delay

with a motto expressing in the fewest and tersest words pos-
sible this national recognition.

It was found that the Act of Congress dated January 18,
1837, prescribed the mottoes and devices that should be
placed upon the coins of the United States. This meant that
the mint could make no changes without the enactment of
additional legislation by the Congress. In December 1863,
the Director of the Mint submitted designs for new one-cent
coin, two-cent coin, and three-cent coin to Secretary Chase
for approval. He proposed that upon the designs either
OUR COUNTRY; OUR GOD or GOD, OUR TRUST
should appear as a motto on the coins. In a letter to the Mint
Director on December 9, 1863, Secretary Chase stated:

I approve your mottoes, only suggesting that on that with the
Washington obverse the motto should begin with the word
OUR, so as to read OUR GOD AND OUR COUNTRY.
And on that with the shield, it should be changed so as to read:
IN GOD WE TRUST.

The Congress passed the Act of April 22, 1864. This legislation changed the composition of the **one-cent coin**
and authorized the minting of the two-cent coin. The
Mint Director was directed to develop the designs for
these coins for final approval of the Secretary. IN GOD
WE TRUST first appeared on the 1864 two-cent coin.

Another Act of Congress passed on March 3, 1865. It allowed the Mint Director, with the Secretary's approval, to place the motto on all gold and silver coins that "shall admit the inscription thereon." Under the Act, the motto was placed on the gold double-eagle coin, the gold eagle coin, and the gold half-eagle coin. It was also placed on the silver dollar coin, the half-dollar coin and the quarter-dollar coin, and on the nickel three-cent coin beginning in 1866. Later, Congress passed the Coinage Act of February 12, 1873. It also said that the Secretary "may cause the motto IN GOD WE TRUST to be inscribed on such coins as shall admit of such motto."

The use of IN GOD WE TRUST has not been uninterrupted. The motto disappeared from the five-cent coin in 1883, and did not reappear until production of the Jefferson nickel began in 1938. Since 1938, all United States coins bear the inscription. Later, the motto was found missing from the new design of the double-eagle gold coin and the eagle gold coin shortly after they appeared in 1907. In response to a general demand, Congress ordered it restored, and the Act of May 18, 1908, made it mandatory on all coins upon which it had previously appeared. IN GOD WE TRUST was not mandatory on the one-cent coin and five-cent coin. It could be placed on them by the Secretary or the Mint Director with the Secretary's approval.

The motto has been in continuous use on the one-cent coin since 1909 and on the ten-cent coin since 1916. It also has appeared on all gold coins and silver dollar coins, half-dollar coins, and quarter-dollar coins struck since July 1, 1908.

A law passed by the 84th Congress (P.L. 84-140) and approved by the President on July 30, 1956, the President approved a Joint Resolution of the 84th Congress, declaring IN GOD WE TRUST the national motto of the United States. IN GOD WE TRUST was first used on paper money in 1957, when it appeared on the one-dollar silver certificate. The first paper currency bearing the motto entered circulation on October 1, 1957. The Bureau of Engraving and Printing (BEP) was converting to the dry intaglio printing process. During this conversion, it gradually included IN GOD WE TRUST in the back design of all classes and denominations of currency.[21]

Seeing that we are in a chapter with a religious theme, I thought it might be interesting to see where your founding fathers stood in relation to their personal beliefs and in "one nation under God."

---

21 https://www.treasury.gov/about/education/Pages/in-god-we-trust.aspx.

Religion of the Signers of the Declaration of Independence[1]			
Name	Place of Birth	Birth	Religion
Adams, John	Quincy, MA	10/30/1735	Unitarian
Adams, Samuel	Boston, MA	9/27/1722	Congregation
Bartlett, Josiah	Amesbury, MA	11/21/1729	Congregation
Braxton, Carter	Newington, VA	9/10/1736	Episcopal
Carroll, Charles	Annapolis, MD	9/19/1737	Roman Catholic
Chase, Samuel	Somerset Co., MD	4/17/1741	Episcopal
Clark, Abraham	Elizabethtown, NJ	2/15/1741	Presbyterian
Clymer, George	Philadelphia, PA	3/16/1739	Quaker/Episcopal
Ellery, William	Newport, RI	12/22/1727	Congregation
Floyd, William	Brookhaven, NY	12/17/1734	Presbyterian
Franklin, Benjamin	Boston, MA	1/17/1706	Deist
Gerry, Elbridge	Marblehead, MA	7/17/1744	Episcopal
Gwinnett, Button	Gloucester, England	1735	Episcopal

Hall, Lyman	Wallingford, CT	4/12/1724	Congregation
Hancock, John	Quincy, MA	1/12/1737	Congregation
Harrison, Benjamin	Charles City Co., VA	4/7/1726	Unknown
Hart, John	Hunterdon Co., NJ	1711	Presbyterian
Hewes, Joseph	Kingston, NJ	1/23/1730	Episcopal
Heyward Jr., Thomas	St. Helena Parrish, SC	7/28/1746	Unknown
Hooper, William	Boston, MA	6/17/1742	Episcopal
Hopkins, Stephen	Providence, RI	3/7/1707	Unknown
Hopkinson, Francis	Philadelphia, PA	10/2/1737	Episcopal
Huntington Samuel	Windham, CT	7/3/1731	Congregation
Jefferson, Thomas	Albemarle Co., VA	4/13/1743	Deist
Lee, Francis Lightfoot	Mt. Pleasant, VA	10/14/1734	Unknown
Lee, Richard Henry	Stratford, VA	1/20/1732	Unknown
Lewis, Francis	Llandaff, Wales	3/21/1713	Unknown

Rush, Benjamin	Philadelphia, PA	1/4/1746	Presbyterian
Rutledge, Edward	Christ Church Parrish, SC	11/23/1749	Anglican
Sherman, Roger	Newton, MA	4/19/1721	Congregation
Smith, James	Northern Ireland	1719	Presbyterian
Stockton, Richard	Princeton, NJ	10/1/1730	Presbyterian
Stone, Thomas	Charles Co., MD	1743	Episcopal
Taylor, George	Ireland	1716	Presbyterian
Thornton, Matthew	Ireland	1714	Presbyterian
Walton, George	Cumberland Co., VA	1741	Anglican
Whipple, William	Kittery, ME	1/14/1730	Congregation
Williams, William	Lebannon, CT	4/18/1731	Congregation
Wilson, James	Carskerdo, Scotland	9/14/1742	Episcopal/Deist
Witherspoon, John	Gifford, Scotland	2/5/1723	Presbyterian
Wolcott, Oliver	Windsor, CT	11/20/1726	Congregation
Wythe, George	Elizabeth City Co., VA	1726	Episcopal

NOTES ON RELIGION:
Congregation is Congregationalist.

Pinning down the religions of some people on this list is notoriously difficult. The "Deist" label, in particular, is a difficult one to assign. The best attempt has been made to assign labels accurately—the assignment can be debated, and this fact is readily acknowledged.

"IN GOD WE TRUST" IN FLORIDA

June 22, 2006, Governor Jeb Bush signed House Bill No. 1145, adopting *In God We Trust* as the official state motto of Florida, effective July 1, 2006. Florida is the only state with this motto.[22]

Your founding fathers were fervent believers in an Almighty God, whom they felt was leading them to form and build a great country. How would they feel today were they to see what is going on not only in government but with your values and in the chaos in the streets and families of America? They surely would not consider it as a blessing from God.

> *"If we ever forget that we are One Nation Under God, then we will be a nation gone under."*
>
> —PRESIDENT RONALD REAGAN

---

22 http://www.netstate.com/states/mottoes/fl_motto.htm.

CHALLENGE

Some author had the nerve to ask me, a retired evangelical pastor, what the challenge should be at the end of a chapter entitled, "In God We Trust! Really!" What a dirty trick!

Let me begin, then, by letting you know that you are going to have to wait a long time for God's blessing on America. So you might as well stop asking for a while and start doing. Asking for a blessing with the state of your affairs is almost an insult. He is probably not listening. You can hope your answer will arrive before hell freezes over!

I would respectfully suggest you do get on your hands and knees and pray.

You don't know how to pray? Find someone who does!

You don't know what to pray? Really! Read the book again; there is plenty of material that you can talk to God about. The founding fathers did!

And pray for what? Not for a blessing right now, but for answers on how to fix all of *your* country's issues that were "made in America."

And the *Good News* is that if the problems were made in America, then the solutions can be found in America by Americans. In my work as a pastor, we talk about the end times that will come one day. My family and I fervently pray that the end times for America are not at hand.

Please join us!

Chapter 8

WHICH WAY AMERICA, NOW?

I thought I would begin this last chapter by sharing with you my personal list of American heroes in random order. I am sure you have some too, and it is probably high time America remembers them on a regular basis.

Look at *Webster*'s definition of *hero*: "A person of distinguished valor or enterprise in danger, or fortitude in suffering; a prominent or central personage in any remarkable action or event; hence, a great or illustrious person."

Jesse Owens	Paul Harvey	Walt Disney
Thomas Edison	Henry Ford	Helen Keller
Colin Powell	Charles Lindberg	Jonas Salk

Abraham Lincoln	Antwone Fisher	Michael Oher
Tyler Perry	Sam Walton	Truett Cathy
Bill Gates	Warren Buffett	Maggie Doyne
Sully Sullenberger	Ron Kovic	Jeffrey Canada
Billy Graham	Ray Robinson	Muhammad Ali
Maya Angelou	Father Gregory Boyle	Bob Hope
Tavis Smiley	Jack Nicklaus	Arnold Palmer
Rosa Parks	Martin Luther King Jr.	Pat Tillman
NASA astronauts	Jackie Robinson	Harriet Tubman
Ronald Reagan	John F. Kennedy	Sitting Bull
Booker T. Washington	Walter Cronkite	Oprah Winfrey
Tony Dungee	Rep. John Lewis	Tecumseh
Katherine Johnson	Dorothy Vaughan	Mary Jackson

If you have journeyed with me since the beginning of this book, let me first of all thank you from the bottom of my heart for being interested—and I hope concerned—enough. I hope you now understand my intentions and hopes, have learned a few things you did not know, and, most of all, have been challenged.

As I leave you, let me say that I believe that I have the moral authority to write this book because my own family and country are at risk. The saying that "what happens in America, stays in America" is supposed to apply to Vegas, but it is simply not (nor has it ever been) true.

On November 19, 1863, President Abraham Lincoln delivered the Gettysburg Address. As a proud Canadian who has been to Gettysburg, I find his speech has touched my heart over the years and today renews my hope in America.

In that speech, he said, "We here highly resolve that these dead shall not have died in vain—that this nation, under God shall have a new birth of freedom—and that the government of the people, by the people, for the people, shall not perish from the earth."

If Honest Abe were president today, that would be his wish as it was then.

Before and since that speech, American men and women have served and died in a war against the British, a Civil War, two great wars, conflicts in Korea and Vietnam, wars in the Middle East, and now, essentially, World War III.

Did they die in vain, as President Lincoln hoped they hadn't back then?

Do those who are serving today deserve a better result in the future?

Is America a better country today than was the one at Gettysburg?

This book has suggested it is not.

As we go to publication, it is the summer of 2016, and election is just months away. For too many months now, we have heard from an abundance of candidates on both sides of the aisle and from one who doesn't even have an aisle.

The caucuses, primaries and conventions are done; it's going to get messy from here on in until only the election night voting remains. *Billions* are being spent by candidates, super PACs, and people like the Koch brothers and other rich Americans. Countless billions of dollars have been spent on advertising, and if you are like me, you have had enough already.

The question for me and the world will be this: How will we feel when we lay our heads down on Tuesday night, November 8, 2016, November 3, 2020, or November 5, 2024?

Will I, for one, once again have tears of joy with great hope and expectations for America, my second-favorite country?

Will we be looking forward to what your next president and the next Congress will accomplish moving forward?

But more important, will the rest of the free world and those who long to be free look to your country to claim the position of leadership it needs to, if we are all to survive?

Protectionism has not worked; numerous intrusions into the affairs of other nations have surely not worked. Sound leadership with a firm resolve, backed by "we the people," to make a positive and crucial impact on the world does.

The time for dysfunction in Washington is over; the time for "you the people" to get your money's worth is now. Stop settling for leadership in government and the financial sector that is not becoming of a potentially great country.

America is *not* the greatest country in the world—but then neither is Canada! There is *no* one greatest country, and, as my daughter has reminded me over the years, "Build a bridge and get over it!"

The final question and challenge for all of you in your journey together as citizens of America is this: "Which way America, now?"

Is history going to repeat itself?

Or is the "new" America and its people going to rise for the second time and take its place among the greatest countries of the world ever?

Do I, as a concerned but always optimistic observer, believe that you will?

"Yes, you can!"

EPILOGUE
THE "TWITTER" PRESIDENT
AND THE "FIRST 100 DAYS"

"TRUMP WINS"

So, after reading this book, you might ask how I felt on the evening of the election? Well, like so many millions around this world, tears came to my eyes once again and this time, they were tears of fear.

I did watch the inauguration and have seen everyone of them since President Kennedy. What an amazing day, and a testament to an orderly transfer of power. But in my humble opinion, what a divisive, classless speech by your president, and a missed opportunity to begin uniting your country.

And then followed the very next day by around the world protests, in over 600 communities on seven continents. Those demonstrations were not only about women's issues, but the fear people and countries have about the new administration's policies.

Americans voted for a change, you needed one and now you have one. And one with a president, who is a by-product of the state of affairs in America today.

And sadly, I believe that the picture of the US flag on this cover is growing brighter.

In the fifties, the US was the most highly regarded country in the free world. What happened? Divisive and partisan politics in America is what happened where everything from city councils to the Supreme Court have been politicized.

And when all is said and done, I am at this point, left with some disturbing questions.

* When will even a few members of Congress vote their consciences on the nomination of cabinet members or any bill of importance?
* Will all Americans watch *The First 48,* or *60 Days In* or *Live PD* and other reality shows, and see the horrible condition the country is in?
* Are you ever going to have legislation on gun safety?
* What about *"the truth, the whole truth and nothing but the truth, so help me"* Trump?
* Why did *"I will release my taxes when I am elected"* end up being, *"I won't release my taxes."*

* Will Turkey move closer to Russia and away from its present alliance with the US?
* Will China become a stronger world trading force because of the cancellation of the TPP and Trump's "America First" stance?
* Will the new administration work with NATO to stop Russian expansion?
* Will this be the beginning of a Trump dynasty? Daughter and or son-in law!
* Who voted in President Steve Bannon and Vice-president Stephen Miller anyway?
* Who will be the first key staff member or cabinet member to leave because of Trump?
* Who will be the first White House support team member (i.e. food services, butlers, maintenance people) to leave because of Trump family?
* Will the aging leadership of both houses of Congress like McConnell and Pelosi step aside? Many have been there past their prime or have forgotten about "we, the people."
* Will a third important party be created because of the dysfunction in Washington and in response to the mess of this election?
* Will the world hold President Assad accountable for the genocide in Syria seeing that he crossed President Obama's line in the sand?
* Will the president bully and coerce the Mexican president or any of the other world leaders into accepting his policies?
* Will the United Nations ever step up and deal with genocides and crazed dictators like Vladimir Putin or Kim

Jong-Un? We all know what happened over 80 years ago when the word "appeasement" was heard.

* Does anyone remember when the US took an isolationist stand before two great wars?

* Will Trump say that he fulfilled most of his campaign promises if he makes it to the next election? Will he then say, " if you give him four more, I'll finish the job?" But at what cost? America cannot afford that price tag.

* Net Mexican immigration is at zero! The GAO (General Accounting Office) estimates the wall will cost 12-15 billion dollars. Would those funds not be better spent on education or health care or infrastructure?

* *"The world is in trouble- but we're going to straighten it out, Ok?"* Trump!

* Will the Republicans loose the Senate and possibly the House in 2018? We all know what happens when that situation occurs in Washington. Nothing happens and nothing gets done! C'mon Congress. Get your act together for the people.

* Is impeachment in the cards for this president?

And then, there were the "first 100 days"

* Signed over 40 executive orders
* No major legislation
* Did someone say, "Russia?"
* Hires good key people at State, Defense, National Security and Homeland
* Muslim travel ban

* Firing of a black woman as chief usher in White House
* Failure to pass new health care bill
* Withdraws US from Trans-Pacific Partnership
* China no longer currency manipulator
* NATO no longer obsolete
* Appointed new supreme court justice
* Launched air strike in Syria
* Played more golf than Obama in first 100 days
* Fires General Mike Flynn
* Does not attend White House Correspondents dinner
* Fires Deputy Attorney General Sally Yates
* Met with several of the top world leaders
* 5 year ban on officials becoming lobbyists and lifetime ban for WH officials
* Approves Keystone pipeline

The next 100 days and beyond will be crucial for America and the world but I almost forgot! On day 111, President Trump fires FBI Director James Comey.

And my next to last question is this. How does President Mike Pence sound? How about President Paul Ryan? How about President Orrin Hatch? And finally, how about President Rex Tillerson? There you have a true succession to President Trump.

My friends, what will we do on July 13th, 2049? Celebrate my 100th birthday, or mourn America as a failed state!

Yes you might!

ABOUT THE AUTHOR

Let's see now! What do these folks really need to know about this guy that they haven't figured out for themselves elsewhere in the book?

The trade says he is supposed to have *qualifications* to write a nonfiction book; well, he doesn't!

He was born in 1949, just across the river from Canada's national capital of Ottawa. This is one of the mainly French-speaking parts of his country, but was raised in a bilingual home. He was doted on by a great mom and a providing father; he was the eldest of five children and surrounded by four wonderful sisters.

He finished high school in 1967 and spent the next two years traveling to many American states and several countries with the musical/educational program called Up with People!

He came back home and spent the next twenty-seven years in the business world.

Since 1999, he has been a pastor of three evangelical Baptist churches in both Canada and the United States. From 2011 until retirement in 2014, he and his wife lived and worked in a suburban community of Phoenix, where they ministered to their last church before returning to Canada.

He has been married to Sharon since 1970, and they have two extraordinary children. Did he mention that he also has two awesome grandsons and a dog?

He is neither Republican nor Democrat nor Independent.

That should be enough!

NOTES ON CHAPTER 2
CHALLENGE

"THE AMERICAN DREAM"

NOTES ON CHAPTER 3
CHALLENGE

"OF EMPIRES AND AMERICA"

NOTES ON CHAPTER 4
CHALLENGE

"HERE'S LOOKING AT YOU!"

NOTES ON CHAPTER 5
CHALLENGE

"FROM MUSKETS TO
WINCHESTERS TO AK-47S"

NOTES ON CHAPTER 6
CHALLENGE

"AND THE AWARD GOES TO…"

NOTES ON CHAPTER 7
CHALLENGE

"IN GOD WE TRUST! REALLY?"